Baby Star Pattern 5 p. 25
   2"

Wrapped Square 3"
   Crossing Pattern p. 42

Square Within a Square #2
   3", bulk   p. 45

Orange Ball — p. 40
   Wrapped bundle 3

Editor:
Jane LaFerla

Art Director:
Thom Gaines

Illustrations:
Hannes Charen

Photographer:
Evan Bracken

Art Assistance:
Chris Bryant

Library of Congress Cataloging-in-Publication Data
Diamond, Anna.
    The Temari book : techniques and patterns for making Japanese
thread balls / Anna Diamond. — 1st ed.
      p. cm.
    ISBN 1-57990-024-0 (hc.)
    1. Fancy work—Japan. 2. Embroidery—Japan. 3. Handicraft—Japan
TT751.D53 1999
746.42—DC21   DD-21155
                                                      CIP

10 9 8 7 6 5 4 3 2 1

First Edition

Published by Lark Books
50 College St.
Asheville, NC 28801, US
©1999, Anna Diamond

For information about distribution in the U.S.,
Canada, the U.K., Europe, and Asia, call Lark Books at 828-253-0467

Distributed in Australia by Capricorn Link (Australia) Pty Ltd.,P.O. Box 6651,
Baulkham Hills Business Centre, NSW 2153,Australia

Printed in Hong Kong

ISBN 1-57990-024-0

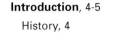

Contents

Introduction

The projects in this book are based on the Japanese craft of Temari, a process that transforms a plain ball into a lovely decorative ornament. By simplifying the traditional techniques of Temari, I've been able to create an easy system for making what I call "embroidered baubles."

I learned how to make these balls when I was living in Malaysia, where some charming Japanese ladies taught me the craft. Though we had no common language, I was able to learn by watching them work. While traditional Temari requires the use of specific patterns and colors, I have designed my own patterns and use a wide range of colors.

Once you master the preliminary steps for preparing a ball and begin working the designs, you will quickly see how you can create many variations from one pattern. Since any pattern will look different with a new color combination, or with altered proportions of colors within a color scheme, you can work a favorite pattern over and over with unique results every time.

In no time, you will have an array of colorful and interesting ornaments to grace a holiday tree, to hang in the window, or to display in a special bowl or basket. The ornaments also make great gifts. And because you're

using readily available, low-cost materials—polystyrene balls, sewing thread, and embroidery thread—only you will know that these exquisitely beautiful spheres cost almost nothing to make.

HISTORY

Originally the balls were constructed from bundles of sweet-smelling herbs and held together with a few threads. Gradually the amount of threads was increased to entirely encase the herbs, and later this was decorated with embroidery. These decorated balls were worked by ladies of the court, then used as playthings to while away the time.

Silken threads were used to make the first balls, but later, when cotton was more widely available, the balls rapidly became more popular. The first balls were called Temari (literally translated as "hand ball") and were used as throwing balls. Later, as the balls became more embellished, they were known as decorative ornaments called Itomari, or "thread ball." In the west, the craft is known as Temari.

With the growing popularity of the craft in Japan, a tradition emerged that continues to be widely practiced today. At the end of the year a mother begins working on a new ball. By New Year's Eve the ball is completed and is placed by the pillow of the youngest girl of the house. On New Year's Day, the girl awakens to find the colorful and thoughtful present.

Today these balls are used more as hangings and decorative objects than as playthings. The centers are often made from unspun cotton or wool that is stuffed into a stocking or thin plastic bag. As the cotton threads are wound around the outside of this stuffed center, they gradually begin to form the shape of the ball. Sometimes a small bell can be incorporated into the center so the ball will jingle when moved.

Another way to form the balls is by using strips of cotton jersey (T-shirt fabric) that are wound around and around each other, all the time pushing and pressing the fabric to form a perfect ball shape. This is very hard to achieve, and it is essential that the finished shape be as symmetrical as possible or the embroidered patterns will be uneven. Using the strips of cotton jersey also produces a heavy ball. Now we are able to buy polystyrene balls, which are lightweight, come in a variety of sizes, and are generally a perfect shape.

HOW TO USE THIS BOOK
While the designs may look complicated when completed, they use logical, point-to-point steps for creating the pattern. If you're not an embroiderer, don't let this hold you back. The design is not made from a series of intricate stitches; in some patterns, the threads that create the design are wrapped around the ball and anchored here and there with one simple herringbone stitch involving no more than a right to left motion.

To begin, read over the basics chapter. It will tell you all you need to know about the materials, including the essentials of working with pins, needles, and embroidery thread. You'll also find the basic techniques for preparing a ball. To see how easy it is, try your hand at wrapping sewing thread around a polystyrene ball to make a base, and at measuring and marking a ball with guidelines to divide it into an even number of sections. Look for the instructions for finishing the ball, including a simple embroidery technique, how to make a loop for hanging, and how to make a tassel.

If you have any further misgivings about your skills, begin by working the first project, Polystar 1 on page 17. It may look elaborate, but is very easy to make. The instructions are planned to give you practice in all the basic techniques. When finished, you'll have a lovely ornament, and will be able to easily progress to the other designs.

Color plays an important part in the designs. The choice is entirely up to you, and you'll find the variations are endless. I've learned that the most effective results are produced by using strong vibrant colors, and also by combining contrasting colors.

Metallic threads will add sparkle and can be used between colored threads or to outline a pattern. Two tones of one color will look quite different if separated by a band of gold or silver thread.

For each project, I've provided the generic color name and the amount of thread used for that project. If you wish to change colors, simply substitute your color choice accordingly. If you can't find a match for the colors by the name I've given them, take this book to your local needlework or craft-supply shop and match the thread to the photographs.

It is my hope that once you feel comfortable with the materials and techniques, you will begin to experiment to create your own designs. One pattern can be completely altered with personal touches, such as highlighting designs with metallic thread, or by incorporating more advanced embroidery stitches to embellish the spaces between the wrapped designs. Most of all, have fun following the patterns. The magic of making these ornaments is in watching the lovely designs emerge as you work.

Basic Materials and Techniques

Materials clockwise: round-head pins, gold metallic thread, pearl cotton (coton perlé) #5, polystyrene ball, scissors, sewing thread, coton á broder, ball, silver metallic thread, pearl cotton #5, needles and sewing thread; center pearl cotton #8

Materials

The following is a guide to the materials you'll need for making the projeu'll be able to find these wherever needlework or craft supplies are sold; craft-supply stores, sewing-supply shops, and the craft departments of general merchandise stores should have what you need. Once you're familiar with the threads suggested here, experiment with a variety of threads in other thicknesses and finishes to create unique, customized effects for your projects.

POLYSTYRENE BALLS

These can be of any size, but should be as perfectly shaped as possible. The most readily available are made of Styrofoam, recognizable by its coarse texture. If you can find them, purchase the slightly denser polystyrene balls that are less porous and have a smoother surface. While the coarse surface of the Styrofoam will not affect the wrapping of the thread, its more porous structure does not hold the pins that mark the points as well as the denser, smoother polystyrene balls.

The best size to start with is a 3-inch (70-80 mm) diameter ball. Exact sizes will vary according to the supplier. If you work with balls that are any smaller in diameter for your first few projects, you may find that they are too small to give you satisfactory results while you're learning the techniques.

Most projects use a 2½-inch (60-65 mm),or a 3-inch (70-80 mm) ball, unless otherwise stated. If you want to work a design on a larger or smaller ball, be aware that you may need to adjust the number of rounds of thread used in making the pattern to accommodate different sizes.

SEWING THREAD

This can be cotton or polyester. Avoid shiny thread, or thread recommended especially for quilting, which has a special finish for gliding through layers of fabric; these threads will be too slippery when used for wrapping a ball. You will need a sufficient length of thread to wind onto the polystyrene ball to completely cover it, plus a little extra to provide enough thickness to hold the stitches of the pattern. It is possible to join threads, but the colors should be identical.

Approximately 275 to 325 yards (250 to 300 m) of sewing thread will wrap a 2½-inch (60-65 mm) or a 3-inch (70-80 mm) ball. For the sake of economy, purchase larger spools of thread. You can find these at manufacturer outlets, odd-lot stores, or you can order them through craft- or sewing-supply catalogs.

METALLIC THREADS

Use any metallic threads that are suitable for hand sewing. Brands such as Guttermans, Goldfingering, Madeira, or Twilleys will work for all projects.

EMBROIDERY THREADS

Start collecting a selection of embroidery threads in bright colors since this will be the palette of colors from which you will work. Use pearl cotton (coton perlé) #5, a twisted two-ply thread, for the larger balls, and pearl cotton (coton perlé) #8, a thinner, twisted two-ply thread, for smaller balls. (Note: You can also use coton á broder, a twisted four-ply thread. It is readily available and widely used in the U.K. It is comparable in size to pearl cotton (coton perlé) #8, but has less sheen.) You may find some shiny yarns that are available. While their bright colors seem to make them an ideal choice for this work, their fiber content and finish make them slippery and thus difficult to use. Note: Never use six-strand embroidery floss.

PINS AND NEEDLES

To plot your points on the ball, you'll need pins with round colored heads. Be sure to buy a variety of colors or a pack with mixed colors. Do not use the long pins suitable for dressmaking; pins that are approximately 1 inch (2.5 cm) long are ideal.

You will need long, sharp needles with eyes that are sufficiently large enough to accommodate the embroidery thread. Darning needles size 1 will give the best results. Avoid using tapestry needles; their rounded points will not move through the wrapped layer of sewing thread as precisely as the embroidery sharps.

Basic Techniques

PREPARING THE BALL

The preparation of the ball—wrapping it with sewing thread, plotting the points, and applying the guidelines—is basically the same for any pattern you will work regardless of the size of the ball. The following directions will take you through each step.

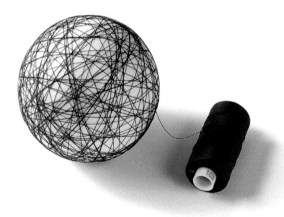

WRAPPING THE BALL

A good base of wound-on thread is essential, both to cover the polystyrene, and to provide a sufficient thickness of thread into which you will stitch the pattern. To begin, first choose the overall color scheme for your pattern. Then select a color of cotton or polyester sewing thread that will be harmonious, either as a contrast or as a background color.

Begin to wind this thread onto the polystyrene ball. Keep winding the thread as *unevenly* as possible. No two threads should lie side by side, or you will find later that the pattern stitches will "slip" beneath the threads. Keep winding until you've completely covered the ball with a firm and dense layer of thread. Unless the wrapping is quite thick, you will find that darker embroidery threads will show through the wound-on thread when you fasten them off.

When you are finished winding, cut the thread off from the spool, leaving a tail approximately 16 inches (40.5 cm) long. Thread the tail onto a needle and sew the tail into the layers of thread that are wrapped around the ball. Take long stitches and catch any loose threads as you go. Fasten off the end by taking a few close and small stitches, cutting off any excess thread.

If you are covering the ball with white thread, it may be difficult to see when the ball is sufficiently covered. To make sure you have enough thickness, wind on a little more white thread than you think you'll need.

PLOTTING THE POINTS

After the ball is wrapped with sewing thread, you will need to mark a grid on the ball that will guide you as you work your chosen pattern. To mark the grid you will need the wrapped ball, paper (standard typing or computer paper works well), scissors, and round-head pins. At this stage, accuracy is of great importance. Since the patterns develop from the division of the ball into even segments, the proper positioning of the grid will determine the outcome of your design.

The following steps are for dividing the ball into eight equal vertical segments. Different patterns may call for dividing the ball into four, six, eight, 10, 12, or 16 equal divisions. For now, work with the following instructions to become familiar with the technique. The diagrams will guide you as you follow each step.

1. Cut a strip of paper ³⁄₈ inch (1 cm) wide by 11 to 12 inches (28-30.5 cm) long. Pin this strip to the ball at any point on the ball's surface. Call this point A. (See figure 1.)

2. Wrap the strip of paper around the widest part of the ball. When it reaches the pin, fold the free end of the strip back away from the pin. Call the fold point B. (See figure 2.) The strip of paper is now pinned to the ball at point A, and has a fold, point B, at the other end. These two points mark the length of the ball's circumference.

3. Make another fold halfway along this strip between point A and point B by taking the fold B and folding it back on itself to the pin at point A. Making sure the strip lies flat against the ball, place a pin in the ball at this spot and call it point C. (See figure 3.) Use the same pin color for marking C as you did for A; when the patterns become more intricate, you will need to easily identify the top and bottom positions. The top and bottom are now marked on the ball. You may need to adjust the position of the pin at point C to make sure it is exactly equidistant from A in all directions. To do this, rotate the folded paper strip on point A, keeping the strip flat against the ball at all times, and adjust the position of the pin at point C accordingly.

4. Take the fold at C and bring it back to A, forming a fold halfway. Call this fold point D (see figure 4). The strip of paper now has four equal divisions.

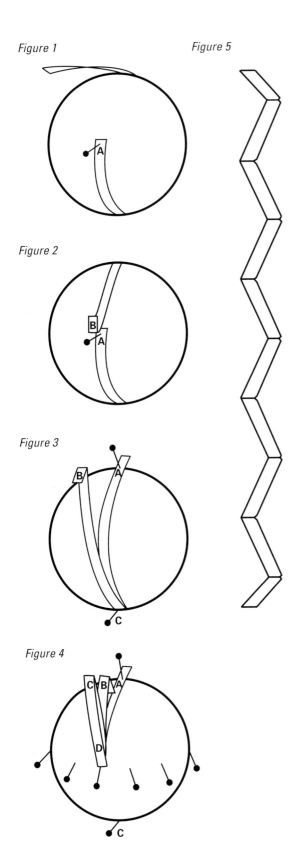

Figure 1

Figure 2

Figure 3

Figure 4

Figure 5

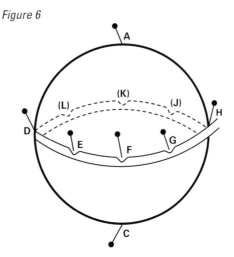

Figure 6

5. You will now begin dividing the ball into the required number of lines using the strip of paper. Turn the ball around, keeping the paper strip from points A to D flat against the ball. As you turn, place a minimum of six pins into the ball to form a ring around the center of the ball. (See figure 4 and the photograph on page 8.) At this stage, you do not need to worry about spacing the pins evenly.

6. Remove the paper strip from the ball, taking care to first place a pin at point A. Fold the strip in half again, making sure all folds are nice and sharp. Using the scissors, cut notches at each fold on one side of the paper strip. Unfold the paper and note that the strip is now divided into eight equal divisions with a little paper left over on each end. (See figure 5.)

7. Lay the paper strip around the ball against the row of pins that you placed around the center. The first and last notches should overlap. Place a pin *opposite* each notch creating the now evenly spaced points D, E, F, G, H, J, K, and L. Remove any extra pins. (See figure 6.) The ball should now have ten pins; one at the top, one at the bottom, and eight equally spaced around the center.

4. Take two small stitches at A to secure the thread. If you don't do this, the threads will come away from the ball when the pins are removed.

5. From the pin at point A, take the needle through the wrapping thread and bring it out at the pin at point D. It may be necessary to take two or three stitches to reach D. Take care to insert the needle into the wrapping thread at the same point from which it exited so the metallic stitches will not show.

6. From the pin at point D, take the metallic thread around the center of the ball, being careful to lay it alongside the pins at points D, E, F, G, H, J, K and L. (See figure 7.) When you've circled the ball, secure the thread at point D with one or two small stitches. To fasten off the thread, take a few long stitches through the wrapping in any direction away from the pin at point D. Cut the excess thread as close to the wrapping as possible. Do not remove the pins at the points; it's helpful to leave them in place, since this will prevent the guidelines from being pulled out of place as you work the pattern.

APPLYING THE GUIDELINES

The last phase in preparing the ball is to apply the metallic thread that creates the guidelines from which you will work the pattern.

1. Take an embroidery needle and a length of metallic thread that will go around the ball at least six times. Thread the needle and make a knot at one end. Insert the needle 3/4 inch (2 cm) from the pin at point A. Take it through the wrapping and out at the pin at point A. Pull the thread so the knot is concealed within the wrapping. Do not pull too hard or the knot will come right through the wrapping, or the thread may break.

2. Wrapping the thread around the ball, take the thread down to the pin at point C, laying it beside the pin at point D, then bring it back to the pin at point A, passing beside the pin at point H. Take a 45° turn around the pin at point A, then take the thread around the ball again as before, laying it beside the pins at points E, C, J, and A.

3. At the pin at point A, take a 45° turn around the pin, then take the thread beside pins F, C, K, and A. Finally, take a 45° turn around the pin at point A and take the thread beside pins G, C, L, and A. The ball is now divided into eight equal, vertical segments.

Figure 7

HOW TO MAKE FOUR, SIX, EIGHT, TEN, TWELVE, AND SIXTEEN VERTICAL SECTIONS

Four: Remove the strip after completing step 5 for Plotting the Points. Do not fold it in half again. Cut notches at the folds on one side of the paper strip. When you open the strip you will see it is divided into four equal sections.

Six: Complete steps 1 to 5 for plotting the points. Remove the strip, taking care to first place a pin at point A on the ball. Fold the strip in half between point A and point B. Divide the folded strip into three equal parts, either by measuring the thirds with a ruler, or by using your eyes as the guide. Cut notches into the folds on one side of the strip and open the strip. You will see it has six equally divided parts.

Eight: Follow steps 1 to 7 for plotting the points.

Ten: Remove the strip, taking care to first place a pin at point A on the ball. Open the strip and use a ruler to measure ten equal sections from point A to point B. Cut notches at these points along one edge of the strip.

Twelve: Follow the directions for making six divisions, then simply fold the strip in half again before cutting the notches.

Sixteen: Fold the strip as for eight divisions, then fold the strip again. Cut notches at these folds before opening.

PLOTTING POINTS FOR PATTERNS WITH MULTIPLE CENTERS

The first section of the book, pages 17 to 61, present patterns worked around two centers. To work them, you basically divide the ball in half and stitch your principal motifs around two centers: point A at the top of the ball, and point C at the bottom. By dividing the ball in other ways, you can create multiple centers which greatly increase design possibilities.

The second section of the book, pages 63 to 126, presents patterns that are worked around four, six, eight, and 12 centers. Just as I've directed you to begin with Polystar Pattern 1 in order to become familiar with the basic techniques, I urge you to work through the Four-Starred Pattern 1 on page 64, to become acquainted with working around more than two centers. You will find that the stitching techniques remain the same; however, plotting the centers and applying the guidelines will be different.

The steps on page 8 and 10 for plotting the points and applying the guidelines, will be all you need for working patterns around two centers. Note that when you complete those steps, except for points A and C, there are only two guidelines crossing at each point. However, patterns worked around more than two centers require that more than two threads cross at selected points as shown in the photograph.

Below are general directions for plotting points for patterns with multiple centers. They will tell you how to apply additional guidelines so that four threads cross at a point to create eight spokes. Individual project instructions will tell you how many guidelines you will need to apply to create the number of spokes needed for that pattern; some instructions call for three threads to cross at a point creating six spokes, some call for six threads to cross at a point creating 12 spokes. For now, work with the following instructions to become familiar with the technique.

1. Complete the steps for plotting the points and applying the guidelines on pages 8 to 10. When completed, you will have ten points marked on the ball, top and bottom and eight around the center.

2. Turn the ball so that the pin at point D becomes the top pin, and points A, K, C, and F become the line around the center. Wrap the paper strip around A, K, C, and F so four of the notches on the strip will correspond to the four pins A, K, C, and F. Place four more pins into the ball at the notches *between* A, K, C, and F.

3. Lay guidelines in metallic thread as in steps 1 to 3 for applying the guidelines. The ball will now have four lines crossing at points D and H, giving eight spokes. Take one or two stitches to secure the thread.

4. Next, turn the ball so the pin at point F becomes the top pin As in step 2 above, wrap the paper strip around A, D, C, and H. Place four more pins into the ball at the notches *between* A, D, C, and H.

5. Following step 3 above, lay the guidelines as before – there will now be four lines crossing at points F and K giving eight *spokes*.

Figure 8

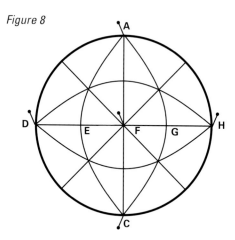

6. The ball will now have six points A, C, D, F, H, and K, each with four threads crossing through them; that is eight spokes at each pin. (See figure 8.) Each of these pins at the points will become the center of a pattern. Remove all the other pins.

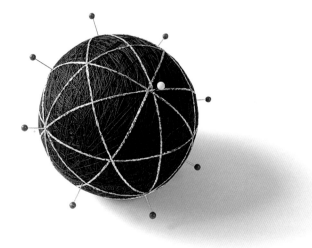

One More Word About Plotting Points

All patterns are plotted according to the preceding directions. The only variation will be in the position of the pins at the centers of the patterns. Some patterns are centered around pins that you place one-third and two-thirds of the distance between the top and bottom pins. The individual project instructions will direct you when you need to do this.

To avoid inaccuracies, use a new strip of measuring paper for each ball. Even the same size balls may have slight, individual variations. You'll also find as you work that the pin holes in the strip will become enlarged. If you place this strip on another ball, you will already be slightly off in your measurement.

The method of placing the pins is always the same since this is the most accurate. With practice, you may be able to place the interim guidelines by eye. However, don't be tempted to do this while you are learning—you will be disappointed with the results in a lopsided or uneven pattern.

Basic Sewing Techniques

Once the ball is prepared, you are ready to begin working your pattern. This will involve using your embroidery thread and needle. I've included some general instructions on sewing that will remain the same for all projects. The basic stitch, the one you will use for most of the projects, is the herringbone stitch and is described in the first project, Polystar Ball 1 (page 19, figure 2-a).

Always work with a manageable length of thread and a long sharp needle. Never double the thread when threading the needle, since a doubled thread can become twisted. Make a small knot at the end of the thread. When you start

with a new thread, use the needle to enter the wrapped layer approximately 3/4 inch (2 cm) away from the point at which you are to begin. Bring the needle to the starting point and gently pull the thread so the knot end is buried under the wrapped layers.

When you run out of thread, or are changing colors, pass the needle under the wrapping thread at the point of exit from the last stitch. Continue under the wrapping thread for approximately ¾ inch (2 cm), then bring the thread to the surface and pull it slightly, cutting the end so the end will retreat back into the layers of the wrapping thread.

Remember when working rounds that you will need to give the stitches enough room so the threads will lie flat and smooth next to each other. The distance between stitches will vary between patterns; in some the stitches need to be close together, and in others there may need to be a space between the rounds of stitching. It's important to always check the individual project instructions for specific directions.

Everyone has an individual "tension" that affects their work. Whether you're knitting, crocheting, embroidering, cross- stitching, or doing needlepoint, this tension distinguishes your work from another's. To get the best results when working on these designs, try to make your stitches as uniform as possible in size and placement. Also, be mindful of the tension of each pattern thread as you work the design. If the threads are too slack or too tight they will affect the subsequent threads and can subtly change the desired effect for the design.

Finishing Techniques

Once you've completed your ornament, you may want to attach a loop for hanging, or use embroidery techniques for decorating the spaces between the pattern threads. I've provided instructions for: Making a simple, decorative knot for hanging; making a tassel; and for making a simple embroidered star motif that works well with the designs.

MAKING A KNOT IN THE HANGING CORD

Figure 9-a

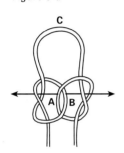

1. Select a cord that matches the colors in the ball, or alternatively make your own twisted cord. A silk cord will add an elegant touch. A crocheted chain makes a good cord, or, make a simple chain using your fingers and one of the threads used on the ball.

Figure 9-b

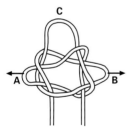

2. Working on a flat surface, form a knot according to figure 9-a. Following figure 9-b, use your finger and thumb to take hold of the two loops at a and b, then pull them in the direction of the arrows, taking care to go over and under the loops as indicated.

Figure 9-c

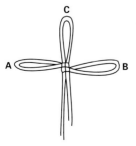

3. Slowly pull a and b so that a firm knot is made at the center, taking care to keep the three loops of equal length as shown in 9-c. Attach the cord to the ball by the loop at c.

A SIMPLE LOOP

1. Take a length of pearl cotton (coton perlé) and fold it in half, creating a loop at one end. Thread both free ends of the thread through the eye of a needle. Use the needle to enter the ball at the desired point of attachment.

2. Bring the needle and two ends through the layer of wrapped thread, then bring the needle through the loop, pulling the ends through the loop to secure the thread. Tie the free ends together, using an overhand knot, and trim any excess thread with scissors.

MAKING A TASSEL

You may decide that your ornament needs a tassel. However, choosing a thread for making a tassel is not easy, since most threads do not hang well. I have found that some metallic threads are the most suitable, or, if you can find it, specialty yarn made especially for making fringe. You may need to experiment with different yarns to find one that will hang well and will match the color scheme of the ornament.

1. Decide on the length of the tassel. Cut a piece of card stock or thin cardboard to that length and wind the yarn around it. When sufficient yarn is wound on the card, cut the end and leave it loose; you will trim it later.

2. Cut two 6-inch (15-cm) lengths of thread. Thread one length around the wound threads at the top of the card, and the other around the wound threads at the bottom. Tie these loosely. Cut two more short lengths of thread, and tie one tightly around the neck of the tassel on one side of the card, and tie the other tightly around the neck on the other side of the card.

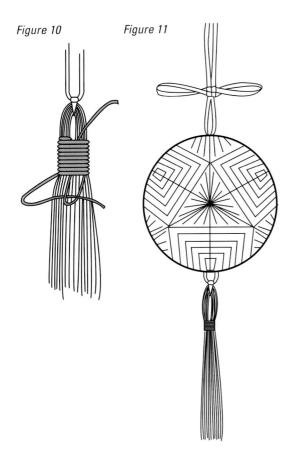

Figure 10　　　*Figure 11*

HANGING THE BALL

To show your pattern to its best advantage, you will need to decide where to attach the cord for hanging. If you sew it on the center of a motif, that motif will not show when the ball is suspended. If your ball has an "equator," a design motif that runs around its center, attach the cord to a point on it; this way, the rest of the pattern will be better displayed.

If you are working with a pattern with squares, attach the cord to the center of the star motif and the tassel to the center of the opposite star motif. Figure 11 shows how this can be done.

STAR MOTIF

A star motif is used frequently to embellish and finish off a design. It is always used in conjunction with other patterns, or to fill in an empty space between patterns, never as the main design on a ball.

Each star motif is worked individually in a fine metallic thread that is the same color as the guidelines. The thread can be the same thickness as the guideline thread, or of a finer weight.

Using surface embroidery stitches, take the metallic thread over and back across the three guidelines at the centers of the shape, until you work a sufficient number of lines to make the star. Secure at the center with two or three small stitches. (See figure 12.)

3. Ease the card out. Cut a 16-inch (40.5-cm) length of thread to whip (wind around) the neck of the tassel. Make a loop at one end of this length and lay the loop on the tassel as indicated in figure 10. Then, beginning at the top of the neck and working down approximately ½ inch (1.5 cm), wind the length around the neck of the tassel. Do not overlap the rounds; be careful to lay each wind of the thread next to the previous round.

4. To fasten off the thread, thread the end into the loop formed in step 3. (See figure 10.) Pull the end of the loop so the whipping thread is secured under the whipping. Thread any loose threads into the tassel and trim the bottom edge to make it even.

Figure 12

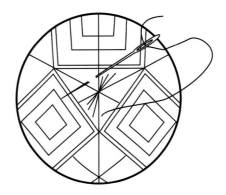

Patterns Around

Two Centers

Polystar Pattern 1

Never hesitate to attempt a design just because it looks complicated. I chose this pattern as the first project because it's really very easy to make. As you follow the instructions, you'll be introduced to the basic methods for creating these ornaments. Once you start working, the simple logic of the geometry, which is the secret to all the patterns, will lead you step by step.

MATERIALS

White Ball

- 3-inch (70-80 mm) ball
- White polyester sewing thread, 270 yards (250 m)
- Gold metallic thread, 13⅓ yards (12 m)
- Pearl cotton (coton perlé) #5, 1 skein = 27.3 yards (25 m), ½ skein each in red, light blue, and dark blue

Pink Ball

- 3-inch (70-80 mm) ball
- Deep pink (rose) polyester sewing thread, 270 yards (250 m)
- Silver metallic thread, 13⅓ yards (12 m)
- Pearl cotton (coton perlé) #5, 1 skein=27.3 yards (25 m), ½ skein each in light blue, medium blue, dark blue, and white

INSTRUCTIONS

1. Wrap the ball and divide it into eight vertical sections with a line around the center. Place pins of one color at points A (top) and C (bottom). Apply the guidelines. Note: You can divide the ball into six, eight, 10, or 12 vertical divisions, with a line around the center. The larger the ball's size, the greater number of vertical segments you'll need. Note, however, that a 3-inch (70-80 mm) ball is too small to divide into more than 12 segments.

Figure 1

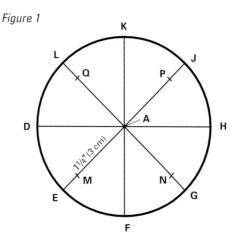

2. Following figure 1, use the strip of measuring paper to plot points that are 1¼ inches (3 cm) from point A on alternate guidelines at points M, N, P, and Q. Place pins on these points.

3. With the needle, which is threaded with a manageable length of thread, begin working as close to point A as possible on guideline AF bringing the thread out to the left of AF. Make the next stitch at N. Working from right to left, take the stitch below the pin, taking the needle beneath guideline AG and through the wrapping threads. Figure 2-a illustrates this stitch, which is a basic herringbone stitch. It is essential that the base of wrapping threads on the ball should be firm and dense, or these stitches will slip.

4. Make the next stitch on guideline AH as close to point A as possible, again taking the stitch from right to left beneath AH and through the wrapping threads. As you continue to stitch, turn the ball counterclockwise with point A at the top, and the point where you're stitching is always toward you. For the next stitch, turn the ball with point A at the top and point P toward you. As you did in step 3, take a stitch below the pin at point P, under the guideline AJ. The next stitch will be on guideline AK as close to point A as possible. Continue around the ball, taking a stitch under each alternate guideline, then a stitch close to point A.

5. Continue with a second round of stitching, keeping the stitches nearest to A as close to the first round as possible. Following figure 2-b, note that the second round of stitches at points M, N, P, and Q should be slightly away from the first round, stitching under the guideline and wrapping thread only. For the stitches close to A, the needle should pass beneath the thread of the first round, as well as beneath the guideline and through the wrapping thread as in figure 2-c. This is essential to achieve the pointed effect. As you work, keep the pins at points M, N, P, and Q in position to ensure that the stitching will not pull the pattern out of shape.

6. Continue working rounds, until the stitching on guidelines AD, AF, AH, and AK comes to within ³⁄₈ inch (1 cm) of the center guideline. Take care as you work to make each stitch as uniform as possible so the pattern will evenly progress toward the center guideline. Keeping the pins in position around the center as you work makes it easier to see that each point of the pattern is the same length. When you are at the designated distance from the center guideline, remove the pins at points M, N, P, and Q

7. Use the strip of measuring paper to plot points that are 1¹⁄₄ inches (3 cm) from point A on alternate guidelines at points R, S, T, and U as shown in figure 3. Using the same colors, work the pattern as before. Begin close to point A on guideline AM, take the next stitch at point S, then close to point A on guideline AN, then the next stitch at point T. Note that this second band will lie on top of one you made in steps 2 to 6. (See figure 4.) Continue stitching in the same color sequence as before, until the second band is within ³⁄₈ inch (1 cm) of the center guideline.

Figure 2-a

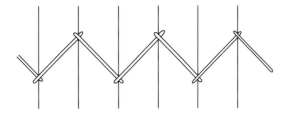

Figure 2-b

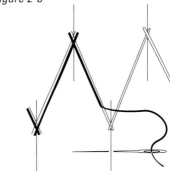

Figure 2-c

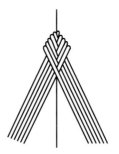

8. Repeat this pattern on the other half of the ball. Turn the ball around so that point C is at the top, then proceed as before in steps 2 to 7. Be careful to begin the work on the same guideline as you did in step 3; for this half, begin on guideline CF, taking the stitch close to C. When you've completed the pattern on the second half, you can remove all pins.

9. To decorate the center between the top and bottom patterns, wrap approximately five rounds of thread to one side of the center guideline, then five rounds to the other side of the center guideline. Begin wrapping the first round close to the center guideline, working away from it toward the points of the star.

10. To hold this wrapped band in place, use the same metallic thread you used for the guidelines to work a herringbone stitch from the points of one star to the other. To make the cross as shown in figure 5, begin from the opposite side of the band and work a second round of herringbone stitch.

Figure 3

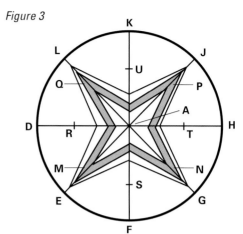

Figure 4

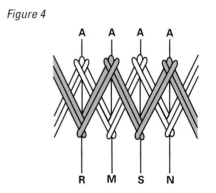

Figure 5

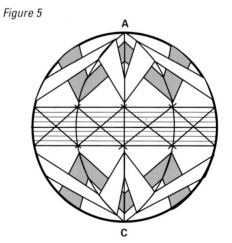

Polystar Pattern 2

The overlapping rounds of thread in this pattern create the design at the point where the bands of color cross. This ball is worked in light and dark shades of pink and purple. Adding a single round of silver metallic thread between every two rounds of colored thread gives this ornament its extra sparkle.

MATERIALS
- 3-inch (70-80 mm) ball
- White polyester sewing thread, 270 yards (250 m)
- Silver metallic thread, 2 yards (2 m)
- Fine silver metallic thread, 5 yards (4½ m)
- Pearl cotton (coton perlé) #5, 1 skein = 27.3 yards (25 m), ½ skein each of dark purple, medium purple, medium pink, and pale pink

INSTRUCTIONS
1. Wrap the ball and divide it into eight vertical sections with a line around the center. Using silver metallic thread, apply the guidelines.

2. Following figure 1, use the strip of measuring paper to plot points that are 1¼ inches (3 cm) from point A on each guideline at points M, N, P, Q, and R, S, T, U. Place pins on these points.

3. You will be working two rounds of dark pink around the first set of points M, N, P, and Q. To begin, bring the threaded needle through the wrapping as close to point A as possible on guideline AD. Take a stitch below the pin at point M, then back to A on guideline AF. Continue counterclockwise around the ball, alternating stitches at points N, P, and Q, with stitches at point A. Work one round in metallic thread. Note: Use the same stitching techniques as described in Polystar Pattern 1, figure 2 on page 19.

4. Work two rounds in dark purple on the second set of points R, S, T, and U. To begin, bring the threaded needle through the wrapping as close to point A as possible on guideline AE. Take a stitch below the pin at point S, then back to A on guideline AG. Continue counterclockwise around the ball, alternating stitches at points T, U, and R, with stitches at point A. Work one round in metallic thread.

5. Return to your starting point on the first set of guidelines, and work two rounds in light pink and one round in metallic thread.

6. Move to the second set of guidelines and work two rounds of light purple, followed by one round of metallic thread.

Figure 1

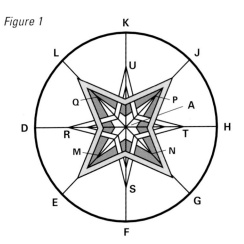

7. Continue working this way until you have four bands of alternating dark and light pink on one set of guidelines, and four bands of alternating dark and light purple on the other set of guidelines. Work a round of the metallic thread between each band of color, then finish with one round of metallic thread. If the pattern at the top of the ball seems too wide, you can work another band to fill the space by stitching from the points of the pattern to a position between the two bands of threads as shown in figure 2.

8. Repeat steps 2 to 7 on the other half of the ball, plotting the two sets of points from point C.

9. To decorate the center, use the dark purple thread to wrap four rounds of thread to one side of the center guideline, then four rounds to the other side of the center guideline.

10. To hold the band in place, use the metallic thread to work a herringbone stitch from the points of one star to the other. To make the cross, begin from the opposite side of the band and work a second round of herringbone stitch. As shown in the photo, a second, larger round of crossed herringbone stitch was worked between the points of the stars.

Figure 2

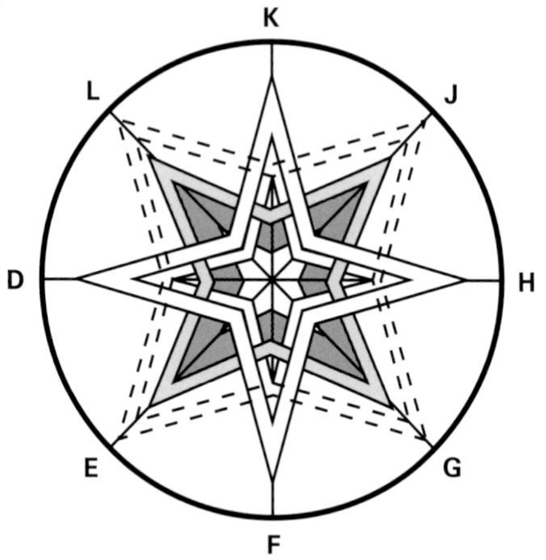

Variation: Using another color combination will give you a different effect. Try working this pattern with two colors. Begin by wrapping the ball with a light blue thread. Using a navy blue and white pearl (perlé) cotton, work two or three rounds of white on the first set of points, then work two or three rounds of navy on the second set of points. Return to the first set of points and work two or three rounds of navy, followed by two or three rounds of white on the second set of points.

> **TIP:** *You don't need to fasten off the thread after each band of color. When you've completed a band, take a small stitch into the wrapping away from the starting point. Leave the needle and thread hanging until you need that color again, then take another small stitch back to the new starting point. You may find that these threads get in the way while you're working the next round. If this bothers you, fasten the thread off after each band of color and start over with a new length of thread.*

Polystar Pattern 3

With this design, you'll see how it's possible to produce a different effect by working one round on the first set of points, then working one round on the second set of points. By working alternately in this way, the bands of the pattern progress simultaneously. Because the ball needs to be divided into 16 vertical sections for working this pattern, I used a 4-inch (100 mm) ball to show this design to its best advantage.

MATERIALS
- 4-inch (100 mm) ball
- Red polyester sewing thread, 433 yards (400 m)
- Silver metallic thread, 4½ yards (4 m)
- Pearl cotton (coton perlé) #5, 1 skein = 27.3 yards (25 m), ¾ skein in white, ½ skein each in light blue, medium blue, and dark blue

working a few rounds in one color, then change to another until the stitching is approximately ³⁄₈ inch (1 cm) from the centerline.

6. Repeat the pattern on the other side of the ball.

7. To complete the pattern wind a few rounds of thread around the center, and finish off with herringbone stitch to hold the band in place as described in step 10 on page 20.

Figure 1

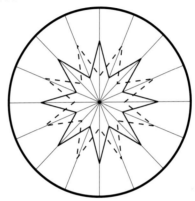

TIP: *If desired, use single rounds of metallic thread between the colored threads to brighten the color scheme. You can use any colors you want for this design. Keep in mind that using the strongest color for the last rounds of the pattern, as shown in the red, white, and blue ball, will emphasize the outline of the shape and will also highlight the intertwining effect.*

INSTRUCTIONS

1. Wrap the ball and divide it into 16 vertical sections with a line around the center. Using metallic thread, apply the guidelines.

2. Use the strip of measuring paper to plot points that are 1¼ inches (3 cm) from point A on each guideline. Place pins on these points.

3. Thread two needles using the same color thread. With one needle, work one round on one set of points as you did for Polystar Pattern 2. Begin as close as possible to point A, then take a stitch below the pin at the point that is 1¼ inches (3 cm) from point A on the next guideline. Continue alternating stitches as you work counterclockwise around the ball.

4. When you've completed the round, leave the needle and thread to the side. Using the other needle and thread of the same color, work the second set of points as you did the first. Figure 1 below shows the position of the points and indicates the stitching pattern for the two threads.

5. Work a few rounds in this manner using one color thread, then change colors. Again, thread two needles using the same color and work a few rounds as described in steps 3 and 4. Continue

Polystar Pattern 4

Notice that the points of the pattern are not all the same length. This will give you extra space to work a larger decoration around the center.

MATERIALS

- 3-inch (70-80 mm) ball
- Blue-green polyester sewing thread, 270 yards (250 m)
- Gold metallic thread, 11 yards (10 m)
- Pearl cotton (coton perlé) #5, 1 skein=27.3 yards (25m), 2/3 skein of red, 1/2 skein of white, 1/4 skein of purple

INSTRUCTIONS

1. Wrap the ball and divide it into eight vertical sections with a line around the center. Using metallic thread, apply the guidelines.

2. Use the strip of measuring paper to plot points that are 1 1/4 inches (3 cm) from point A on alternate guidelines. Follow figure 1 on page 18 for Polystar Pattern 1 to guide you. Call these points M, N, P, and Q.

3. Using two or three colors, work a wide band of approximately 10 rounds by alternating stitches from point A to points M, N, P, and Q as you work counterclockwise around the ball. After

working so many rounds, the shape formed at the top of the pattern close to A becomes quite wide and will prevent you from working an identical band on a second set of points, as you have in the previous projects.

4. Following figure 1, plot points V, W, X, and Y approximately 1 1/4 inches (3 cm) from point A on guidelines AD, AF, AH, and AK. Next, move points M, N, P, and Q closer to point A until they are 1/2 inch (1.5 cm) away from A on guidelines AE, AG, AJ, and AL.

5. Beginning at point V, and working counterclockwise, stitch from V to M, M to W, W to N, N to X, X to P, P to Y, Y to Q, and Q to V. Work six rounds on these points, changing colors and adding a round of metallic thread as desired.

Figure 1

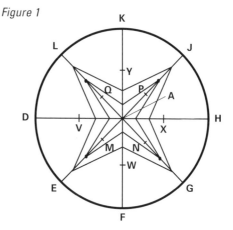

Figure 2

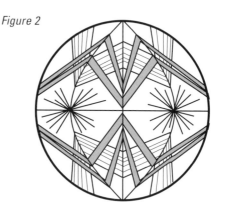

6. Decorate the center with a wrapped band that is held in place with the crossed herringbone stitch as described in the previous projects. Or, use the space formed by the uneven points to work a star motif as shown in figure 2.

> **TIP:** As for the previous projects, the stitches closest to point A should always be worked closer together than those at the outer points of the pattern as shown in figure 2 on page 000. Remember, when working polystar patterns, you are always working from point A or C down toward the centerline.

Polystar Pattern 5

This pattern, which is relatively quick to work, looks very attractive on smaller 1½- or 2-inch (40- or 50-mm) balls. (When working on smaller balls, remember to use a finer thread.) You'll find that the stitches, which stretch from point A to below the center guideline, are longer than in other patterns. Be careful, though; if you make the stitches too long, the curve of the ball will prevent them from lying close together.

MATERIALS

Red and Green Ball

- 1½- or 2-inch (40- or 50-mm) ball
- Red polyester sewing thread, 163 yards (150 m)
- Silver metallic thread 2½ yards (2 m)
- Rayon thread (viscose); used here Anchor Marlitt, skein = 11 yards (10 m), 2 yards (2 m) each in light blue, white, and medium green

Red and Blue Ball

- 1½- or 2-inch (40- or 50-mm) ball
- Red polyester sewing thread, 163 yards (150 m)
- Silver metallic thread, 2½ yards (2 m)
- Pearl cotton (coton perlé) #8, 5⅓ yards (5 m) each in white, light blue, and dark blue

INSTRUCTIONS

1. Wrap the ball and divide it into eight vertical sections with a line around the center. Using metallic thread, apply the guidelines. For this pattern, you will not need to plot any more points with pins, since you can judge the distance below the centerline by eye. You will find it helpful, however, to keep all eight pins around the centerline as you work.

2. Following figure 1, begin stitching on guideline AD as close to A as possible. Take the thread to point E, which is on the centerline, and take a stitch from right to left at E below the centerline. Then bring the thread back to point A on guideline AF and take a stitch as close to point A as possible. Take the thread to point G, and take a stitch from right to left below the centerline. Working counterclockwise around the ball, continue taking stitches at point A, then on alternate guidelines on points just below the centerline.

3. Work the second, and all subsequent rounds, as you did in step 2. Six rounds in various colors will probably be sufficient. The pattern will progress away from the center guideline into the lower half of the ball.

4. Continuing on the top half of the ball, work an identical band of six rounds beginning on guideline AE as close to point A as possible. Take the thread to point F (see figure 1), and make a stitch from right to left just below the centerline as you did in step 2 for the previous band. Then bring the thread back to point A on guideline AG, and take a stitch as close to A as possible. Take the thread to point H, and take a stitch from right to left just below the centerline. Working counterclockwise around the ball, continue taking stitches at point A, then on alternate guidelines on points just below the centerline.

5. Turn the ball around so that C is at the top, and repeat the pattern as you did in steps 2 to 4. The points of the pattern will overlap the threads already worked and form a diamond shape where they cross, as shown in figure 2.

Variation: You can create a different pattern around the center by working alternate bands on the top and bottom. To do this, begin using your first color to work a band of color on the top of the ball around point A, then use the same color to work a band of color on the bottom around point C. Return to the top and continue with your second color, then work the second color on the bottom. Continue to work alternate bands until the pattern is complete.

> **TIP:** When working with the rayon thread, thread the needle with two strands. As you work, be careful that the threads do not twist.

Figure 1

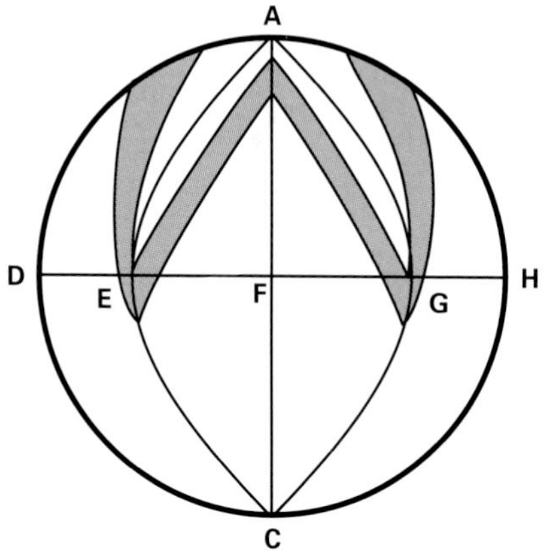

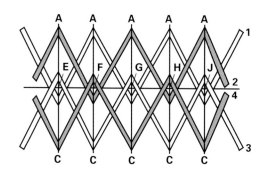

Figure 2

Polystar Pattern 6

This sample is worked in three colors: one for the stitching around point A, the second for the stitching around point C, and the third for the pattern around the center. If you are undecided about which colors to use, choose shades of the same color for the stitching around points A and C, then use a bright contrast for the center motif. The effect will be harmonious and handsome.

MATERIALS

- 2- or 2½-inch (50-65 mm) ball
- Royal blue polyester sewing thread, 163 yards (150 m)
- Fine gold metallic thread, 2½ yards (2 m)
- Rayon thread (viscose), used here Anchor Marlitt, skein = 11 yards (10 m), 1 yard (1 m) in deep pink, 4½ yards (4 m) each in light blue and turquoise

INSTRUCTIONS

1. Wrap the ball and divide it into 12 vertical sections with a line around the center. Using metallic thread, apply the guidelines.

2. Using your first color, and following figure 1, begin stitching close to point A on guideline AD. Bring the thread down to point E, taking the next stitch right to left at E just below the centerline. Bring the thread up to point A on guideline AF and take a stitch. Bring the thread to point G, take a stitch and then back to A. Continue working around the ball counterclockwise, alternately taking stitches at point A, then on points just below the centerline on alternate guidelines. Complete one round.

3. Turn the ball so point C is at the top. Using the second color, repeat step 2 around point C. Begin by stitching close to point C on guideline CD. Bring the thread down to point E, taking the next stitch right to left at E just below the centerline. Bring the thread up to point C on guideline CF and take a stitch. Bring the thread to point G, take a stitch and then back to C. Continue working around the ball counterclockwise, alternately taking stitches at point C, then on points just below the centerline on alternate guidelines. Complete one round.

Figure 1

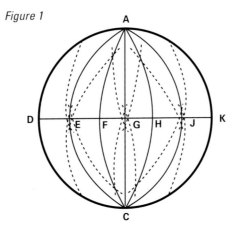

4. Return to point A and work a second round, then a second round at point C. Continue alternating top and bottom as you stitch each subsequent round. When you make the stitches at points A and C, make them gradually wider so the threads will fill the open spaces between guidelines. However, keep the stitches that you take at the points below the centerline small and close together.

5. Using the third color, fill the spaces between the stitching around the centerline with vertical stitching as shown in figure 2.

Figure 2

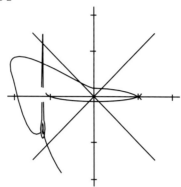

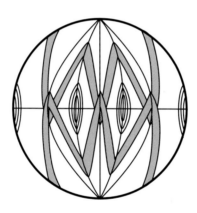

> **TIP:** *When working with the rayon thread, thread the needle with two strands. As you work, be careful that the threads do not twist.*

Polystar Pattern 7

This project was worked on a 2½ inch (60-65 mm) ball with polyester thread for the wrapped base and two strands of rayon thread worked as one for the stitching.

MATERIALS

- 2½ inch (60-65 mm) ball
- Rose (mauve) polyester sewing thread, 217 yards (200 m)
- Silver metallic thread, 3⅓ yards (3 m)
- Rayon thread (viscose); used here Anchor Marlitt, skein = 11 yards (10 m), 1 yard (1 m) of light green, 6½ yards (6 m) each of turquoise and deep rose

INSTRUCTIONS

1. Wrap the ball and divide it into 10 vertical sections with a line around the center. Using metallic thread, apply the guidelines.

2. Following figure 1, plot points 1 to 10 by placing pins on each guideline ½ inch (1.5 cm) from the centerline. Plot points 11, 12, 13, 14, and 15 on guidelines AD, AF, AH, AK, and AM by placing pins ⅜ inch (1 cm) above the pins on points 1, 3, 5, 7, and 9.

3. Using two different colors of rayon thread, thread two needles, each with two strands of the

Figure 1

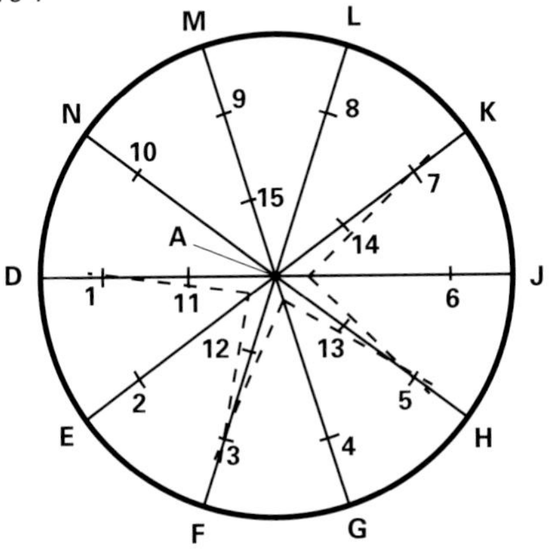

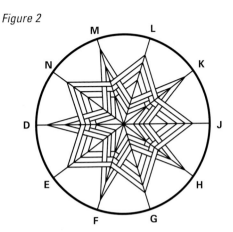

Figure 2

same color. With the first color, begin stitching at point 1 on guideline AD, then bring the thread close to point A on guideline AE. Take a stitch, right to left, at point A, then bring the thread to point 3 on guideline AF. Working counterclockwise around the ball, continue taking stitches at point A, then on alternate guidelines at the numbered points that are ½ inch (1.5 cm) from the centerline until you've completed one round.

4. With the other needle threaded with two strands of the second color, begin at point 11 on guideline AD, then take a stitch at 2 on AE. Bring the thread to point 12 on guideline AF, take a stitch, then bring the thread to point 4 on AG. Continue counterclockwise in this way around the ball until you've completed one round.

5. Return to the first needle with the first color and repeat step 3. Remember, when taking the stitches close to points A and C, take the needle *under* the previous rounds and through the base wrapping threads as shown in figure 2-c on page 19.

6. Using the second color, repeat step 4. Remember, when taking a stitch at points 11, 12, 13, 14, and 15 *do not* take the needle underneath the previous round, but make the stitch a fraction below the previous one as shown in the photograph.

7. Following figure 2, continue to work this pattern first around point A, then likewise around point C, until there is approximately a ⅜ inch (1 cm) space at the center between the long points of the top and bottom star.

8. Make a band around the center by winding a few rounds of thread around the ball to fill the space between the long points of the top and bottom star. Use a crossed herringbone stitch to hold the band in place.

9. Add a star motif (see page 15) on the top and bottom between the guidelines at points A and C.

> **TIP:** *You don't want the two threads worked as one to get twisted; make sure they lie side by side.*

Polystar Pattern 8

In this pattern, you'll be taking two stitches on the same guideline. The slight asymmetry that this gives the design creates a sense of subtle movement.

MATERIALS

- 3-inch (70-80 mm) ball
- Turquoise polyester sewing thread, 325 yards (300 m)
- Silver metallic thread, 5⅓ yards (5 m)
- Fine silver metallic thread, 8½ yards (8 m)
- Pearl cotton (coton perlé) #5, 1 skein=27.3 yards (25 m), ½ skein of red, ⅓ skein of black

INSTRUCTIONS

1. Wrap the ball and divide it into eight vertical sections with a line around the center. Using metallic thread, apply the guidelines.

2. Following figure 1, plot points M, N, P, and Q, placing the pins 1¼ inches (3 cm) from point A. Plot points 1, 2, 3, and 4, placing the pins close to point A.

3. Beginning at point M, take the thread to point 2 close to point A on guideline AF, and take a stitch right to left. Take the thread to point N and take a stitch. Take the thread to 3 on AH and take a stitch. Take a stitch at P on AH. Take a

stitch at 4 on AK. Take a stitch at Q on AK. Take a stitch at 1 on AD. Take a stitch at M on AD. Continuing to work this way around the ball, complete four to six rounds.

4. Following figure 2 reposition the pins, moving them counterclockwise to the next guidelines (those that have not been worked).

Figure 1

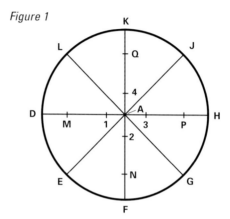

Figure 2

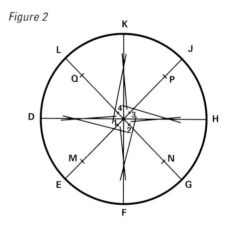

5. Repeat step 3 on the repositioned points.

6. Repeat steps 2 to 5 on the other half of the ball.

7. To make the pattern around the center, follow figure 3. Plot the points x and y on every other guideline. Note that x is close to the stitching of the top pattern, and y is approximately ¼ inch (.5 cm) from the bottom pattern. Stitch from x to *y* on the same guideline. Stitch from *y* to *x*, skipping the guideline in between. Stitch from x to y on this guideline. Continue stitching this way around the ball until you've worked approximately four to six rounds.

8. When you've completed the rounds in step 7, move the pins at *x* and *y* counterclockwise to the next guidelines and repeat the pattern, working

2. Following figure 1, plot points that are halfway between the centerline and point A on each guideline. Place pins on these points. Beginning with guidelines AD, call them 1, 3, 5, 7, 9, 11, 13, 15, 17, 19, 21, 23, 25, 27, 29, and 31. Plot points that are halfway between the points plotted above and point A on each guideline. Place pins on these points. Beginning with guideline AE, call them 2, 4, 6, 8, 10, 12, 14, 16, 18, 20, 22, 24, 26, 28, 30, and 32. *Note:* While I've used many numbered points to describe this pattern, you may find it easier to work the stitches by placing some of them by eye.

Figure 3

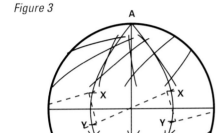

Polystar Pattern 9

Because the pattern divides the ball into 16 sections, this design should be worked on a larger ball. This project was worked on a 3½-inch (85-90 mm) ball, but would also look good on a 4-inch (100 mm) ball.

MATERIALS

- 3½- (85-90 mm) or 4-inch (100 mm) ball
- White polyester sewing thread, 379 yards (350 m)
- Silver metallic thread, 16 yards (15 m)
- Pearl cotton (coton perlé) #5, 1 skein = 27.3 yards (25 m), 1 skein each in medium magenta, navy blue, and purple

INSTRUCTIONS

1. Wrap the ball and divide it into 16 vertical sections with a line around the center. Using metallic thread, apply the guidelines.

3. To begin stitching, again follow figure 1. Enter the wrapped layer with the needle and thread so the needle exits just to the left of point 1 on guideline AD, then take the thread to point 2 on guideline AE. Following figure 1, take a stitch, right to left, at point 2, taking the needle through the wrapping threads so it exits close to point A on guideline AD. Next, take the thread to point 3 on AE and take a stitch. Take a stitch at 4 on AF, taking the needle through the wrapping threads so it exits close to point A on guideline AE. Take the thread to point 5 on AF and take a stitch. Take a stitch at point 6 on AG, taking the needle through the wrapping so it exits close to point A on AF. Take the thread to point 7 on AG and make a stitch. Make a stitch at point 8 on AH, taking the needle through the wrapping so it exits close to point A on AG. Continue working in this way as you move counterclockwise around the ball.

4. Complete enough rounds, changing colors as desired, to bring the stitching within ⅜ to ¾ inch (1-2 cm) of the centerline.

5. Repeat steps 2 to 4 around point C.

6. To decorate the center between the top and bottom patterns, wrap a band of thread around the centerline. To hold the band in place, stitch over the band following figure 2. Begin the stitching at point 1, just left of the guideline, then take a right to left stitch at 2, then a stitch at 3. Continue to work this way, moving counterclockwise around the ball.

Figure 1

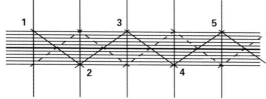

Figure 2

Polystar Pattern 10

This pattern divides the ball into 15 vertical sections. As you can see from the photograph, the uneven number of divisions creates a swirl effect for this design. This ball was worked on a 3½-inch (85-90 mm) ball and can also be worked on a 3- or 4-inch (70-80 or 100 mm) ball.

MATERIALS

- 3-, 3½-, or 4-inch (70-100 mm) ball
- Light blue-green polyester sewing thread, 379 yards (350 m)
- Gold metallic thread, 5⅓ yards (5 m)
- Pearl cotton (coton perlé) #5, 1 skein=27.3 yards (25 m), ¼ skein of white, ½ skein each of medium green and red

INSTRUCTIONS

1. Wrap the ball and divide it into 15 vertical divisions with a line around the center. To divide the ball into 15 divisions, follow the instructions for dividing the ball into 10 divisions, explained on page 11. Instead of measuring 10 equal divisions from point A to point B, measure 15. Using metallic thread, apply the guidelines.

2. Following figure 1, plot the points by placing pins ¾ inch (2 cm) from the centerline on all

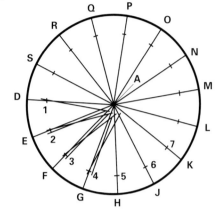

Figure 1

Figure 2

vertical guidelines. Call the point on guideline AD point 1.

3. To begin stitching, again follow figure 1. Enter the wrapped layer with the needle and thread so the needle exits just to the left of point 1 on guideline AD. Make the next stitch as close as possible to point A on AF. Take the thread to point 2 on AE and make a stitch. Make a stitch as close as possible to A on AG. Take the thread to point 3 on AF. Make a stitch as close as possible to A on AH. Take the thread to point 4 on AG. Continue working this way as you move counter-clockwise around the ball.

4. Complete enough rounds to bring the stitching within ⅜ inch (1 cm) of the centerline.

5. Repeat steps 2 to 4 around point C.

6. To decorate the center between the top and bottom patterns, wrap a band of thread around the centerline. To hold the band in place, stitch over the band following figure 2. Begin the stitching at point 1, just left of the guideline, then take a right to left stitch at 2, then a stitch at 3. Continue to work this way, moving counter-clockwise around the ball.

Polystar Pattern 11

Repositioning the points as you work creates this interlocking pattern. As with Polystar Patterns 9 and 10, work this pattern on a larger ball to highlight the design. As shown, the pattern was worked on a 4-inch (100 mm) ball.

MATERIALS

- 4-inch (100 mm) ball
- Light blue polyester sewing thread, 433 yards (400 m)
- Silver metallic thread, 16 yards (15 m)
- Pearl cotton (coton perlé) #5, 1 skein = 27.3 yards (25 m), ⅔ skein each of dark blue and maroon

INSTRUCTIONS

1. Wrap the ball and divide it into 16 vertical sections with a line around the center. Using the metallic thread, apply the guidelines.

2. Following figure 1, plot the first set of points. Place pins ½ inch (1.5 cm) from point A on alternate guidelines; then, on the remaining guidelines (those in between), place pins 1 inch (2.5 cm) from point A. Work two rounds on these points as you did for Polystar Pattern 1 (page 100), stitching from one pin to the next.

3. Following figure 2, remove the pins and reposition them so the pins that were ½ inch (1.5 cm) from point A on alternate guidelines are now 1 inch (2.5 cm) from point A; and the ones that were 1 inch (2.5 cm) from point A are now ½ inch (1.5 cm) from point A. Work two rounds on these pins.

4. Following figure 3, remove the pins and reposition them 1 inch (2.5 cm) from point A on alternate guidelines. Note that these pins should be within the previous round of stitching to allow the next two rounds to overlap the first two rounds. Position the other pins 1½ inches (3.5 cm) from point A on the remaining guidelines. Work two rounds on these pins.

Figure 1

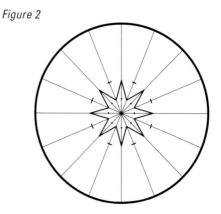

Figure 2

5. Remove the pins and reposition them so the pins that were 1 inch (2.5 cm) from point A on alternate guidelines are now 1½ inches (3.5 cm) from point A; and the ones that were 1½ inches (3.5 cm) from point A are now 1 inch (2.5 cm) from point A. Work two rounds on these pins.

6. Continue to remove and reposition the pins further from point A, then work two rounds. Note that each set of two rounds must overlap the previous rounds.

7. When the rounds reach almost to the center line, turn the ball over and work steps 2 to 6 around point C.

8. Work two sets of rounds around the center of the ball. Note that the top and the bottom points will overlap the stitching already worked on the top and the bottom half of the ball.

Figure 3

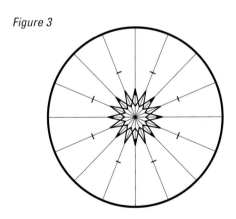

TIP: *To highlight a round, add rounds of silver thread as desired.*

Crossed Polystar Pattern

Similar to the polystar patterns, this motif is worked in a much different way. The design crosses over the centerline, forming a pattern at the center as well as at the top and bottom.

MATERIALS

- 3-inch (70-80 mm) ball
- Light blue polyester sewing thread, 325 yards (300 m)
- Silver metallic thread, 11 yards (10 m)
- Pearl cotton (coton perlé) #5, 1 skein = 27.3 yards (25 m), ½ skein each of light blue and emerald green, ¾ skein of dark blue

INSTRUCTIONS

1. Wrap the ball and divide it into 12 vertical sections with a line around the center. Using metallic thread, apply the guidelines.

2. Following figure 1, plot points around the ball by placing pins 1½ inches (4 cm) away from points A and C on every guideline.

3. Again following figure 1, enter the wrapped layer with the needle and thread so the needle exits just to the left of and below the pin at point 1. Take the thread up toward point A and take a stitch, right to left, at point 2. Take the thread down toward point C and take a stitch, right to left, at point 3. Take the thread up toward point A and take a stitch, right to left, at point 4. Continue taking stitches on every other guideline as above, as you work counterclockwise around the ball to complete one round.

4. Following figure 2, work a second and third round, placing the stitches above and below the first round so the points of the motif will gradually move closer to points A and C. Note that the threads cross over the previous rounds at the centerline. Continue working in this way until the stitching is approximately ⅜ inch (1 cm) from points A and C.

5. Using the same color sequence, repeat steps 3 and 4 on all the guidelines between those already worked.

6. If you find it necessary to secure the threads where they cross over the centerline, take two or three stitches using a matching thread.

Figure 1

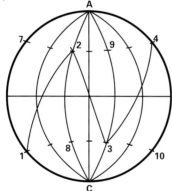

Figure 2

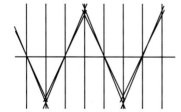

Square Crossing Pattern 1

Square crossing patterns get their name from the square that is formed by alternately crossing bands of thread across the top and bottom points of the ball. This pattern, and the ones that follow, are worked around two centers. On page 123, you'll find a ball that uses the same stitching technique to develop a simple design.

MATERIALS

- Light Turquoise Ball
- 3-inch (70-80 mm) ball
- Light turquoise polyester sewing thread, 325 yards (300 m)
- Gold metallic thread, 4⅓ yards (4 m)
- Fine gold metallic thread, 4⅓ yards (4 m)
- Pearl cotton (coton perlé) #5, 1 skein = 27.3 yards (25 m), ½ skein each of mauve, medium blue, light blue, light turquoise

INSTRUCTIONS

1. Wrap and divide the ball into eight vertical sections with a line around the center. Using metallic thread, apply the guidelines.

2. Following figure 1, plot points H, J, K, and L by placing pins halfway between points A and D, A and E, A and F, and A and G.

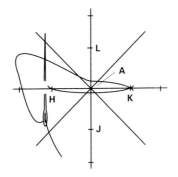

Figure 1

3. To begin stitching, again follow figure 1. Enter the wrapped layer with the needle and thread so the needle exits to the left of and just below point H on guideline AD. Lay the thread along the right side of the guideline DF. Turn the ball around so that AF is toward you, and take a stitch from right to left just below K. Lay the thread along the right side of the guideline FD. Turn the ball around so that AD is toward you, and take a stitch from right to left just below H. Note: Always turn the ball so that the point at which you are stitching is toward you.

4. Repeat step 3 once or twice more.

Figure 2

5. Following figure 2, rotate the ball so that guideline AE faces toward you. Enter the wrapped layer with the needle and thread so the needle exits to the left of and just below point J on guideline AE. Proceed as in steps 3 and 4.

6. Continue in this way, working alternately on DF and EG until this stitching reaches the points D, E, F, and G on the centerline.

7. Turn the ball over and repeat this pattern on the other side, working around point C until the points of the motifs meet at the centerline. Be sure to begin stitching on the same guidelines as before.

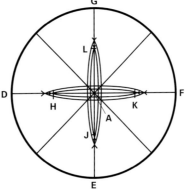

8. You can decorate the spaces between the motifs in two ways. One way is shown in figure 3. Place two pins on the same vertical guideline, spacing each pin approximately ⅜ inch (1 cm) from the centerline. Work as described above. Move the pins so they are on the centerline, spacing each pin approximately ⅜ inch (1 cm) from the vertical guideline and work as above. (You can also choose to work only on the vertical guideline.) Another way is to decorate the spaces between the motifs with the star motif using metallic thread.

Figure 3

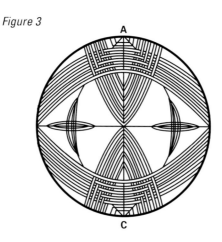

Variation: You can achieve different effects for this pattern by varying the number of rounds worked in step 4 before stitching in the other direction. You'll find that one round worked in each direction will look quite different than a pattern where three or four rounds are worked in each direction.

Square Crossing Pattern 2

Extending the points of the motif below the centerline, and working each motif on alternate guidelines, creates this variation of the square crossing pattern.

MATERIALS

- 3-inch (70-80 mm) ball
- Medium pink polyester sewing thread, 325 yards (300 m)
- Silver metallic thread, 4⅓ yards (4 m)
- Pearl cotton (coton perlé) #5, 1 skein = 27.3 yards (25 m), ¼ skein of light blue, ½ skein each of medium purple, medium blue, and dark blue

INSTRUCTIONS

1. Wrap the ball and divide it into eight vertical sections with a line around the center. Using metallic thread, apply the guidelines.

2. Following figure 1 on page 37, plot points H, J, K, and L by placing pins halfway between points A and D, A and E, A and F, and A and G.

3. To begin stitching, again follow figure 1 on page 37. Enter the wrapped layer with the needle and thread so the needle exits to the left of and just below point H on guideline AD. Lay the thread along the right side of the guideline DF. Turn the ball around so that AF is toward you, and take a stitch from right to left just below K. Lay the thread along the right side of the guideline FD. Turn the ball around so that AD is toward you, and take a stitch from right to left just below H. Note: Always turn the ball so that the point at which you are stitching is toward you.

4. Repeat step 3 once or twice more.

5. Following figure 2 on page 37, rotate the ball so that guideline AE faces toward you. Enter the wrapped layer with the needle and thread so the needle exits to the left of and just below point J on guideline AE. Proceed as in steps 3 and 4.

6. Continue working in this way, alternating rounds on DAF and EAG, until the stitching reaches approximately ¾ inch (2 cm) below the centerline into the lower half of the ball as shown in figure 1.

7. Turn the ball over and repeat this motif on the other side around point C, working the pattern on the guidelines in between those used for the motif worked around point A. As shown in figure 2, the threads will cross over each other at point C, and the two points of the pattern will reach approximately ¾ inch (2 cm) below the centerline into the other half of the ball. Note that there should be an even gap of approximately ½ inch (1.5 cm) between the pattern around point A at the top and around point C at the bottom where the wrapping threads show through.

> **TIP:** If you find that the outer round of thread is slipping off the ball, take a few invisible anchoring stitches through the wrapping layer to secure the outer thread.

Figure 1

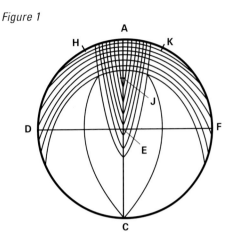

Figure 2

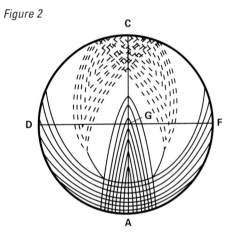

Square Crossing Pattern 3

This is a variation on Square Crossing Pattern 2. The motifs around points A and C are worked until they completely cover the ball.

MATERIALS

- 3-inch (70-80 mm) ball
- Yellow polyester sewing thread, 325 yards (300 m)
- Gold metallic thread, 5½ yards (5 m)
- Pearl cotton (coton perlé) #5, 1 skein = 27.3 yards (25 m), ¾ skein each of lime green, yellow, dark green, and medium rose

INSTRUCTIONS

1. Follow steps 1 through 7 for Square Crossing Pattern 2 on pages 38 and 39. Work the motifs consecutively. Work one color around point A, then the same color around point C before changing to the next color. Following rounds will be worked first around A, then around C.

2. It is essential that the stitching around point A and around point C is on alternate guidelines so the patterns will not meet at the centerline. Continue stitching until the patterns meet, and the wrapping thread is completely covered.

3. To finish the ball, and to prevent any threads from slipping off, follow figure 1. Plot points 1, 2, 3, and 4 around point A by placing pins at the edge of the square pattern. Stitch a few rounds from 1 to 3 and from 2 to 4. Repeat on the bottom of the ball around point C.

Figure 1

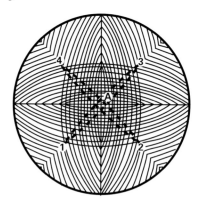

Square Crossing Pattern 4

This is a variation of Square Crossing Pattern 1. Plotting the points one quarter of the way on the guidelines, rather than halfway, creates a larger square where the threads cross.

MATERIALS

- 3-inch (70-80 mm) ball
- Dark blue-green polyester sewing thread, 325 yards (300 m)
- Gold metallic thread, 10½ yards (10 m)
- Fine gold metallic thread, 4⅓ yards (4 m)
- Pearl cotton (coton perlé) #5, 1 skein = 27.3 yards (25 m), ⅓ skein of mauve, ½ skein each of red and purple

INSTRUCTIONS

1. Wrap the ball and divide it into eight vertical sections with a line around the center. Using a metallic thread, apply the guidelines.

2. As in figure 1 on page 37 for Square Crossing Pattern 1, plot points H, J, K, and L on guidelines AD, AE, AF, and AG. However, instead of placing the pins halfway on the guidelines, place the pins, one quarter of the way from point A to D, A to E, A to F, and A to G.

3. Follow steps 3 through 6 on page 37 for Square Crossing Pattern 1. You may find it necessary to place some extra pins in the ball to stop any threads from slipping off.

4. Following figure 1, carefully place pins 1, 2, 3, and 4 at the outer corners of the square, measuring the distance between pins to make sure that they are equidistant from point A. Using the same stitching pattern, stitch from points 1 to 3 and points 2 to 4.

5. Repeat steps 2 to 4 around point C.

6. To finish, work the star motif between points D, E, F, and G around the center of the ball.

Figure 1

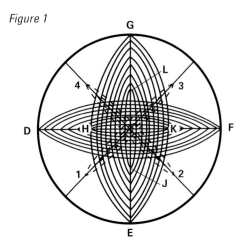

Wrapped Square Crossing Pattern

In this pattern, you work both motifs simultaneously by winding threads around the ball. You can make this pattern on a ball that has been divided into either four or six vertical sections—the way you work them will be exactly the same. A ball with six vertical sections will have three motifs crossing at the top and the bottom. This project was worked on a ball with four sections.

MATERIALS

- 3-inch (70-80 mm) ball
- Dark turquoise polyester sewing thread, 325 yards (300 m)
- Silver metallic thread, 8⅔ yards (8 m)
- Pearl cotton (coton perlé) #5, 1 skein = 27.3 yards (25 m), ½ skein each of pink, dark pink, and maroon.

INSTRUCTIONS

1. Wrap the ball and divide it into four vertical sections with a line around the center. Using metallic thread, apply the guidelines.

2. Follow figure 1, which shows a front view of the ball. Note that point F, which is not shown on figure 1, is on the opposite side of the ball and corresponds to point D. Begin at point D.

Enter the wrapped layer with the needle and thread so the thread exits just above the center guideline at point D to the left of the guideline. Lay the thread on the left of guideline DAF. At point F, cross over the guideline and lay the thread to the right of the line FCD. At this point, the thread will have made a circle around the ball, completing one round. Rotate the ball in your hand as you lay the thread. Work one more round.

Figure 1

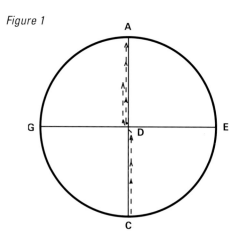

3. Using the same thread, cross over the guideline at point D and lay the thread alongside DAF to the right of the guideline. At F, cross over the guideline and lay the thread to the left of the guideline FCD. Complete two rounds of thread on each side of the guideline DAFC.

4. Following figure 2, turn the ball so that guideline AEC is facing toward you. Repeat steps 2 and 3, this time beginning at point E and working alongside guideline EAGC.

5. Return to guideline DAFC and work bands of a different color as you did in steps 2 and 3, beginning at point D, and working around guideline DAFC.

6. Return to guideline EAGC and work bands of the same color as in step 5, working as in step 2 and 3, beginning at point E, and working around guideline EAGC.

7. Continue in this way, changing colors as desired, until you form large squares at points A and C.

8. Finish off the design with star motifs worked around the center of the ball in the spaces between the points. It will be necessary to secure the threads where they cross over the guidelines at points D, E, F, and G. One way to do this is to use the metallic thread and take a cross-stitch over the threads.

Figure 2

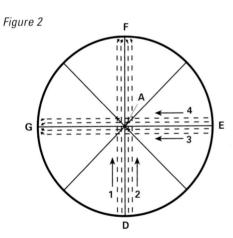

Square Within a Square Pattern 1

This project combines design elements that have already been discussed to create a new pattern. The solid mass of color around points A and C, with expanding points of the polystar patterns, creates motifs that radiate from the top and bottom. This project was worked on a smaller, 2-inch (50 mm) ball using the thinner pearl cotton (coton perlé) #8 (coton á broder).

MATERIALS
- 2-inch (50 mm) ball
- Medium blue polyester sewing thread, 190 yards (175 m)
- Gold metallic thread, 6½ yards (6 m)
- Pearl cotton (coton perlé) #8 (coton á broder), 15 yards (14 m) each of red and dark lime green

INSTRUCTIONS
1. Wrap the ball and divide it into 16 vertical sections with a line around the middle. Using metallic thread, apply the guidelines.

2. As shown in figure 1, stitch a square around A. Enter the wrapped layer with the needle and thread so the needle exits close to point A, just to the left of guideline SA. Take the thread to guideline FA and take a stitch, right to left. Take the thread to guideline KA and take a stitch, right to left. Take the thread to guideline OA and take a stitch, right to left. Then take the thread back to guideline SA, entering the wrapped layer just to the right of the guideline. Work four rounds.

3. As you did for step 2, stitch a second set of rounds on guidelines DA, HA, MA, and QA to make a second square. Note that this round will overlap the corners of the first square that you stitched in step 2.

4. On each set of guidelines, stitch six sets of squares, beginning each set with one round of gold thread. Alternate stitching the squares from guidelines SA, FA, KA, and OA, to guidelines DA, HA, MA, and QA.

5. Following figure 2, plot points 1, 2, 3, and 4 on guidelines AS, AF, AK, and AO by placing pins halfway between the corners of the square and the center guideline.

6. Following the stitching for the polystar patterns, and referring to figure 2, enter the wrapped layer with the needle and thread so the needle exits at the corner of the square on guideline DA, just to the left of the guideline. Take a stitch, right to left, at point 2 on guideline FA. Continuing to work counterclockwise around the ball, take a stitch at the corner of the square on HA. Take a stitch at 3 on KA. Take a stitch at the corner of the square on MA. Take a stitch at 4 on OA. Take a stitch at the corner of the square on QA. Take a stitch at 1 on SA. Take a stitch at the corner of the square on DA. Repeat this step until the stitching reaches the center guideline

7. Replot points 1, 2, 3, and 4 on guidelines DA, HA, MA, and QA. Repeat step 6, working on the guidelines in between.

8. Repeat steps 2 to 7 around point C.

Figure 1

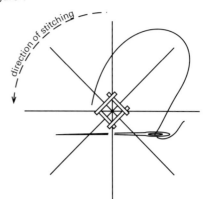

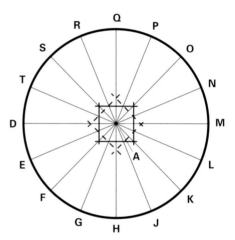

Figure 2

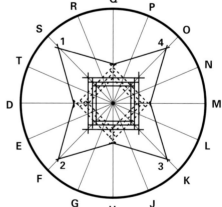

Circle of Diamonds
Square Within a Square
Pattern 2

The overlapping rounds at the center of this design create a circle of diamonds around the middle of the ball. For an easy variation of this pattern, stitch octagons around points A and C instead of the squares.

MATERIALS
- 3-inch (70-75 mm) ball
- Red polyester sewing thread, 325 yards (300 m)
- Silver metallic thread, 9 yards (8 m)
- Pearl cotton (coton perlé) #5, 1 skein = 27.3 yards (25 m), ¾ skein each of dark green, medium blue, and white

INSTRUCTIONS
1. Wrap the ball and divide it into 16 vertical sections with a line around the center. Using metallic thread, apply the guidelines.

2. Begin by stitching a square around point A. To do this, take a stitch on every fourth guideline, keeping the stitches close to point A. Work four or five rounds.

3. Change your thread color and stitch a square on the middle guidelines between those worked in step 2. Work the same number of rounds as in step 2.

4. Change your thread color and stitch a square on the first guidelines worked in step 2, working the same number of rounds. Change your thread color and stitch a square on the same guidelines as those in step 3, working the same number of rounds. Continue working this way until the corners of the squares are one-third to halfway between point A and the centerline.

5. Following figure 1, plot points 1, 3, 5, 7, 9, 11, 13, and 15 by placing pins ½ inch (1.5 cm) from the centerline. Plot points 2, 4, 6, 8, 10, 12, and 14 by placing pins approximately 1¼ inches (3 cm) from the centerline. For accuracy, check that each set of points is the same distance from point A. You may need to adjust the pins slightly.

6. Stitch as you would in a polystar pattern. Enter the wrapped layer with the needle and thread so the needle exits to the left of guideline AD, just below the pin at point 1. Take the thread to point 2 and take a stitch, right to left. Take a stitch at point 3, then point 4. Continuing to work counterclockwise around the ball, work as many rounds as are needed to almost reach the centerline.

Figure 1

7. Repeat steps 2 to 6 around point C.

8. Move points 2, 4, 6, 8, 10, 12, and 14 to the guidelines between those already worked around point A by placing pins approximately 1¼ inches (3 cm) from the centerline.

9. Working the polystar pattern, take a stitch at point 2, then take the next stitch below the center on the next guideline. Take a stitch at point 4, then take the next stitch below the center on the next guideline. Continue working counterclockwise around the ball in this way. Work two rounds.

10. Repeat step 8 and 9 around point C. These stitches will overlap the stitches of the step 9.

11. Continue to alternate every two rounds between the points around point A and the points around point C until you've worked six rounds on each set of points. If desired, add an additional round of metallic thread to highlight the design.

Hexagonal Tristar 1

Like the polystar patterns, this design has identical motifs that you work on the top and bottom of the ball. Unlike the polystars, you'll find that patterns worked around two centers with a central square, pentagon, or hexagon, use stitching patterns that form the threads into a solid mass of color around points A and C.

MATERIALS

- 3-inch (70-80 mm) ball
- Medium lavender polyester sewing thread, 325 yards (300 m)
- Silver metallic thread, 2¼ yards (2 m)
- Fine silver metallic thread, 3⅓ yards (3 m)
- Pearl cotton (coton perlé) #5, 1 skein=27.3 yards (25 m), ⅓ skein each of pink, deep rose, purple, and red

INSTRUCTIONS

1. Wrap the ball and divide it into six vertical sections with a line around the center. Using the metallic thread, apply the guidelines.

2. Following figure 1, plot points K, L, and M on guidelines AD, AF, and AH, placing the pins approximately 1¼ inches (3 cm) from point A.

3. To begin stitching, again follow figure 1. Enter the wrapped layer with the needle and thread so

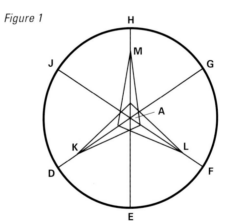

point 2 on AG to 5 on AJ; from point 5 on AJ to 1 on AE. This forms the first round.

7. Repeat step 6, changing colors as desired. Continue with the rounds until the points of the pattern almost reach the centerline.

8. Turn the ball so that point C is at the top. Repeat steps 2 through 7. In order to make an exact mirror image of the pattern on this side of the ball, you must begin stitching on guideline CD, which corresponds to guideline AD in step 2.

9. To finish off, wrap a band of threads around the center of the ball. Then work two rounds of the herringbone stitch to hold the band in place. Or, you can work a star motif on points D, F, and H.

the needle exits just to the left of guideline AD close to point A. Take the thread to point L on AF and take a stitch right to left. Take a stitch close to A on AH, then at K on AD. Take a stitch close to A on AF, then at M on AH. Take a stitch close to A on AD. This completes the first round. Note that you have worked twice around the ball to form this pattern.

4. Repeat step 3, changing colors as desired. A hexagon shape will develop at the top around point A with three points on guidelines AD, AF, and AH. Continue with the rounds until the points of the pattern almost reach the centerline. This completes the first motif. Remove the pins, then continue.

5. Make the second motif that overlaps the first. To begin, follow figure 2 to plot points 1, 2, and 3, placing the pins approximately ⅜ inch (1 cm) from the center on guidelines AE, AG, and AJ. Plot points 4, 5, and 6 by placing pins at three corners of the hexagon as shown.

6. To begin stitching, again follow figure 2. Enter the wrapped layer with the needle and thread so the needle exits just to the left of guideline AE close to point 1. Take the thread to 4 on AG and take a stitch. Continue to work as follows: from point 4 on AG to 3 on AJ; from point 3 on AJ to 6 on AE; from point 6 on AE to 2 on AG; from

Figure 1

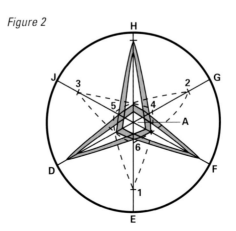

Figure 2

Hexagonal Tristar 2

This is a variation of Hexagonal Tristar 1. For this pattern you'll make a small central hexagon first before extending the points.

MATERIALS

- 3-inch (70-80 mm) ball
- Red polyester sewing thread, 325 yards (300 m)
- Silver metallic thread, 14 yards (13 m)
- Fine silver metallic thread, 3¼ yards (3 m)
- Pearl cotton (coton perlé) #5, 1 skein = 27.3 yards (25 m), ½ skein each of green, purple, and light blue

INSTRUCTIONS

1. Wrap the ball and divide it into six vertical sections with a line around the center. Using the metallic thread, apply the guidelines.

2. Following figure 1, work a solid mass of threads around point A to form a hexagon. To do this, enter the wrapped layer with the needle and thread so the needle exits just to the left of guideline AD and very close to point A. Take the thread to guideline AE and take a stitch very close to point A. Take the thread to guideline AF, and take a stitch very close to point A. Continue taking a stitch close to point A at each guideline as you work counterclockwise around the ball.

3. Continue working several rounds of thread until the hexagon extends approximately ⅜ inch (1 cm) from point A.

4. Plot points K, L, and M on guidelines AD, AF, and AH, placing the pins approximately 1¼ inches (3 cm) from point A. Plot points N, P, and Q by placing pins on guidelines AD, AF, and AH at the edge of the stitched hexagon. Following figure 1, and as you did for Hexagonal Tristar 1, stitch from point K to point P. Then from P to M, M to N, N to L, L to Q, and Q to K. Repeat until the points reach the centerline.

Figure 1

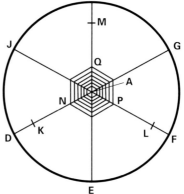

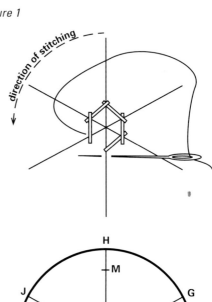

5. The hexagon may be so large that it becomes impossible for you to fit any more stitches, preventing the points extending from K, L, and M from reaching the centerline. With this pattern, you could work a few rounds to extend the points as shown in figures 2 and 3.

6. Repeat steps 2 through 5 on the other half of the ball around point C.

7. To finish the design, work the star motif around the center in the spaces between the points of the pattern.

Figure 2

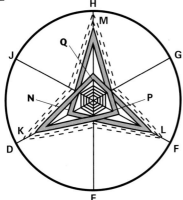

Figure 3

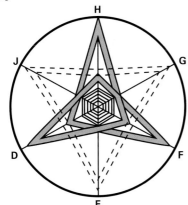

Hexagon Within a Hexagon

Utilize the way the pattern weaves the threads around the top and bottom points by selecting rich, jewel-like colors for a dramatic presentation.

MATERIALS

- 3-inch (70-75 mm) ball
- Light blue polyester sewing thread, 325 yards (300 m)
- Silver metallic thread, 3 yards (2.5 m)
- Pearl cotton (coton perlé) #5, 1 skein = 27.3 yards (25 m), ½ skein each of red, medium emerald green, and purple

INSTRUCTIONS

1. Wrap the ball and divide it into 12 vertical sections with a line around the center. Using metallic thread, apply the guidelines.

2. Following figure 1, begin by stitching a hexagon around point A. To do this, take a stitch on every other guideline, keeping the stitches close to point A. Work four rounds.

3. Change your thread color and stitch a hexagon on the guidelines between those worked in step 2. Work two rounds. Change color again and stitch two more rounds on the original guidelines.

4. Following figure 1, alternate in this way until the stitching reaches to within 1 inch (2.5 cm) of the center guideline.

5. Repeat this pattern around point C, being careful to begin stitching the hexagon on the same vertical guideline as in step 2.

6. Following figure 2, plot points 1 to 6 by placing pins ½ inch (1.5 cm) above the center guideline. Plot points 7 to 12 by placing pins ½ inch (1.5 cm) below the center guideline. For the first round, stitch from point 1 to 9, 9 to 5, 5 to 7, 7 to 3, 3 to 11, and 11 to 1. For the second round, stitch from point 2 to 10; 10 to 6; 6 to 8; 8 to 4; 4 to 12; and 12 to 2. Repeat these two rounds four or five more times. If desired, work the star motif in the spaces around the center of the ball.

Figure 1

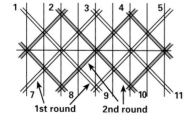

Figure 2

1st round   2nd round

TIP: *You can vary this pattern by making wider bands of each color in steps 3 to 5. In the project shown in the photograph, I worked a wider band of a third color (red) halfway through the pattern.*

Pentagon Star

Begin by stitching a pentagon as the central motif, then follow the pattern to create this lovely star. This design exposes more of the wrapping layer, so be sure to choose a color of sewing thread that will highlight the pattern threads.

MATERIALS
- 3-inch (70-80 mm) ball
- Orange polyester sewing thread, 325 yards (300 m)
- Gold metallic thread, 11 yards (10 m)
- Pearl cotton (coton perlé) #5, 1 skein = 27.3 yards (25 m), ¼ skein of olive green, ½ skein each of yellow and red

INSTRUCTIONS
1. Wrap the ball and divide it into 10 vertical sections with a line around the center. Using metallic thread, apply the guidelines. Do not remove any of the pins.

2. Following figure 1, stitch a pentagon around points A and C. To do this, take a stitch on alternate guidelines as close to the pins at points A and C as possible. Work four or five rounds.

3. Again following figure 1, plot points J, K, L, M, and N on guidelines AD, AE, AF, AG, and AH. To do this, use the paper strip as your guide by

placing one notch at A. Lay the strip along the guidelines above, and place the pins for the points at the next notch. The pins should be at the same distance from point A on the guidelines as the distance between the guidelines around the center.

4. Following figure 2, begin stitching. Enter the wrapped layer with the needle and thread so the needle exits just below the pin at Point J and to the left of guideline AD. Working counter-clockwise around the ball, take a right to left stitch at L, then at N, then at K, then at M, then back at J. This completes one round of the pattern. Stitch six rounds, always taking the stitches below the pins at the points and changing colors as you wish.

5. Again following figure 2, place pins O, P, Q, R, and S on the guidelines in between the points plotted in step 3. This time, place the pins halfway between point A and the center guideline.

6. As you did in step 4, begin stitching at the pin at point O, then take a stitch at Q, then at S, then at P, then at R, then back at O. This completes one round of the pattern. Stitch three or four rounds, always taking the stitches below the pins at the points.

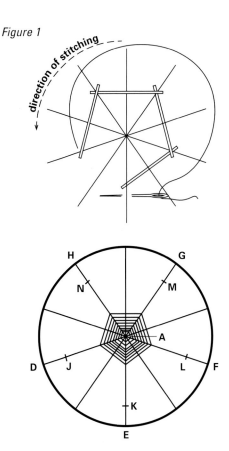

Figure 1

Figure 2

Figure 3

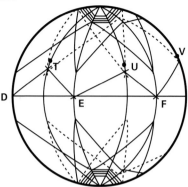

7. Return to the first set of points plotted in step 3. As you did in step 4, work three more rounds on these points.

8. Remove all pins, except those around the center. Following figure 3, plot points T, U, V, W, and X by placing the pins in the spaces that are just *within* the stitching on the second set of guidelines. Note that points W and X are not shown in the diagram since they are on the other side of the ball.

9. Again following figure 3, enter the wrapped layer so the needle and thread exits just below the center guideline at point D, and just to the left of guideline AD. Take the thread to point T and take a stitch, right to left. Continue working counterclockwise around the ball taking a stitch at E, then at U, then at F, then at V, then at G, then at W, then at H, then at X. Stitch 5 or 6 rounds.

10. Repeat steps 3 to 9 on the other half of the ball, working around point C. Note that the stitching in step 9 will cross over the centerline, creating a diamond shape where the rounds from the top and bottom overlap.

11. To finish, follow figure 4. Place the pins for points 1 and 2 on all the unstitched guidelines,

positioning the pins approximately ¾ inch (2 cm) above and below the centerline. Enter the wrapped layer so the needle and thread exits to the left and just below the pin at point 2. Lay the thread alongside the right of the vertical guideline. Then turn the ball so point 1 is facing toward you. Below the pin at point 1, take a stitch from right to left. Turn the ball so point 2 is facing you and take a stitch. Repeat working in this way around points 1 and 2 until sufficient rounds have been worked. Repeat this stitching around the ball on all points 1 and 2.

Figure 4

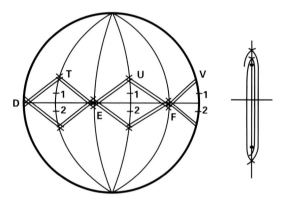

Overlapping Triangles

Begin this design by stitching a hexagon as the center of the motif. Then, working round by round in three different colors, you will make the overlapping triangles that create this interlocking pattern.

MATERIALS

- 3-inch (70-80 mm) ball
- Blue-green polyester sewing thread, 325 yards (300 m)
- Silver metallic thread, 5½ yards (5 m)
- Pearl cotton (coton perlé) #5, 1 skein = 27.3 yards (25 m), ¾ skein each of white and dark rose, ½ skein of navy blue

INSTRUCTIONS

1. Wrap the ball and divide it into six vertical sections with a line around the center. Using metallic thread, apply the guidelines.

2. Following figure 1, begin stitching at point A and work around all six guidelines to create a hexagon of approximately 10 rounds.

3. The rest of the stitching will be made in a triangular shape. You will work row by row using 3 needles, each threaded with a different color. Each round will overlap the previous rounds. To begin, thread three needles, each with a different color. Following figure 1, enter the wrapped layer with one of the needles and navy blue thread so the needle exits just left of guideline AD, and a little way from the hexagon as shown in figure 1. The thread will pass one of the points of the hexagon made in step 2. Take a second stitch on AF. Take a third stitch on AH, then complete the triangle on AD. Note: The distance from point A on AD where you begin stitching depends on the size of the hexagon. As shown in the diagram, you want the thread to touch the points of the hexagon on lines AE, AG, and AJ as you work around the ball.

4. With the second needle (threaded with dark rose), and following figure 1, begin stitching on guideline AE. Take a second stitch on AG, a third on AJ, then complete the triangle on AE. Note: The distance from point A on AE where you begin depends on the size of the hexagon. As shown in the diagram, you want the thread to touch the points of the hexagon on lines AF, AH, and AD as you work around the ball as you did in step 3.

5. Continue to alternately work these two triangles until you complete three rounds of each color.

6. Introduce the third color (as shown, white). Stitching as in steps 3 and 4, work three rounds of the third color, alternating with three rounds of dark rose. Note: The second color (as shown, dark rose) will continue to be worked as in step 4 throughout the pattern.

7. Go back to the first color (as shown, navy blue) and work as in step 6, completing three rounds worked alternately with three rounds of dark rose. Continue to alternate the first and third colors with the second color until the points of the motif reach almost to the centerline as shown in figure 2.

8. Repeat steps 2 through 7 on the other side of the ball around point C.

9. To finish, work star motifs around the centerline to fill in the spaces between the points of the motifs. If you find that any of the threads on the last round are slipping off the ball, use a matching thread to take a tiny stitch at the center of the thread to keep the round in place.

Figure 1

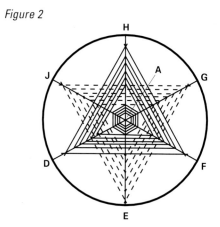

Figure 2

TIP: *For extra sparkle, I used one round of metallic thread after working every three rounds of the first and third colors in steps 6 and 7. By doing this, the last round is worked in a metallic thread which adds a nice highlight to the design.*

Stars and Diamonds

The diamonds encircling the sphere offset the stars that form around points A and C. Work this on a smaller 2½ inch (60-65 mm) ball for a delicate look.

MATERIALS

- 2½-inch (60-65 mm) ball
- Medium rose (fuchsia) polyester sewing thread, 217 yards (200 m)
- Gold metallic thread, 5½ yards (5 m)
- Fine gold metallic thread, 22 yards (20 m)
- Pearl cotton (coton perlé) #5, 1 skein = 27.3 yards (25 m), ¼ skein each of white, green, blue, and red

INSTRUCTIONS

1. Wrap the ball with the sewing thread, then wrap it with the fine metallic thread, allowing the colored thread to show through. Divide the ball into eight vertical sections with a line around the center. Using the metallic thread, apply the guidelines.

2. Following figure 1, plot points D, E, F, G, H, J, K, and L. For points E, G, J, and L, place pins on alternate guidelines at one-third the length of the guideline from point A to point C. Note that points J and L are on the other side of the ball. For points D, F, H, and K, place pins approximately ¼ inch (.75 cm) below the centerline.

3. Again following figure 1, begin stitching at point D by entering the wrapped layer with the needle and thread so the needle exits to the left of the guideline and just below the pin. Take the thread beside pin E, on the right side of the guideline, up to point A, then down to point J, which is on the other side of the ball.

4. Take a stitch at K, then take the thread around the pin at point L, laying it beside the guideline to the right, and bring the thread up to A. Then take the thread down to G, bringing it around the pin.

5. Take a stitch at H, then take the thread around the pin at point J, laying it beside the guideline to the right, and bring the thread up to A. Then take the thread down to E, bringing it around the pin.

6. Take a stitch at F, then take the thread around the pin at point G, laying it beside the guideline to the right, and bring the thread up to A. Then take the thread down to L, bringing it around the pin, and take a final stitch at D.

7. Following figure 2, and as you did in step 2, plot additional points by placing pins on the guidelines in between those already worked. Repeat steps 3 through 6 on these guidelines.

8. Repeat steps 3 through 7 on the other half of the ball. Repeat the pattern until sufficient rounds have been completed.

9. Following figure 3, work a herringbone stitch around the center of the ball. This stitching will go beneath the threads at points D, F, H, and K on both sides of the center guideline.

Figure 1

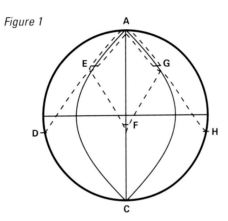

Figure 2

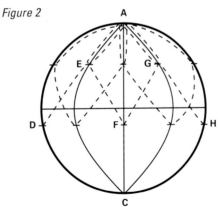

Figure 3

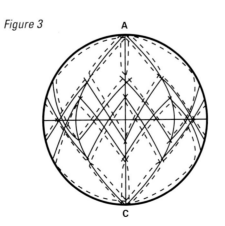

Wrapped Star Crossing Pattern

As with wrapped patterns, this design is not created by stitching the threads in place at specified points. To make this motif, you wrap three different colors of thread around the ball. The stars are formed by the threads that cross over points A and C.

MATERIALS

- 3-inch (70-80 mm) ball
- White polyester sewing thread, 325 yards (300 m)
- Silver metallic thread, 6½ yards (6 m)
- Fine silver metallic thread, 6½ yards (6 m)
- Pearl cotton (coton perlé) #5, 1 skein = 27.3 yards (25 m), ¾ skein each of light blue, medium blue, and dark blue

INSTRUCTIONS

1. Wrap the ball and divide it into six vertical sections with a line around the center. Using metallic thread, apply the guidelines.

2. You will be working with three different colors and a silver thread at the same time. To determine the length for each thread, measure the length required to wind thread around the ball eight times. Cut three lengths of each color to this measurement, plus a little extra for fastening off.

3. Following figure 1, which shows a top view of the ball, wrap two rounds around the ball diagonally on each side of DAGCD, crossing the thread over at guidelines D and G.

4. Repeat step 3 on guideline EAHCE and then on guideline FAJCF, as shown in figure 1.

5. Continue wrapping two rounds on each side of the guidelines, with a round of silver in between, until the central hexagons that are formed around points A and C are each approximately 1¼ inches (3 cm) across.

6. To finish, you will need to hold the threads together where they cross at the center of the ball. To do this, wrap a thin band of threads around the center; or, take a few cross-stitches at each crossing point. Work the star motif around the center in the spaces between the motifs.

Figure 1

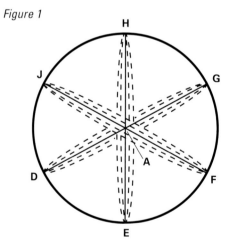

TIP: *Use a strong or dark color thread, or metallic thread, for the last round of wrapping in step 5 to emphasize the shapes formed at points A and C.*

2. Following figure 1, take the strip and mark the halfway points between points A and C and points C and B. Divide each of these two sections (A to C and C to B) into eight equal divisions, as shown in figure 1. For accuracy, measure the spacing for the dots with a ruler. When completed, you should have two sets of eight dots on the strip, each approximately ¼ to ⅜ inch (.75 cm) apart.

Wrapped Bands 1

Don't throw away the paper measuring strip once you've divided the ball. For this design, adding additional marks to the strip will provide you with extra help for accurately winding the pattern thread around the ball.

Figure 2

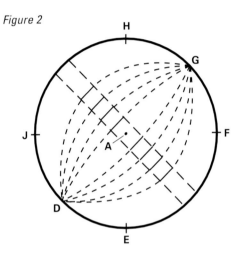

MATERIALS

- 3-inch (70-80 mm) ball
- Light blue polyester sewing thread, 325 yards (300 m)
- Silver metallic thread, 6½ yards (6 m)
- Pearl cotton (coton perlé) #5, 1 skein = 27.3 yards (25 m), ¾ skein of dark red, ¼ skein each of mauve, purple, and red

INSTRUCTIONS

1. Wrap the ball and divide it into six vertical sections with a line around the center. Note: Do not apply the vertical guidelines. Just keep the pins and the guidelines around the center to mark the sections.

3. Following figure 2, lay the strip of paper across the ball and pin it in place.

4. Using metallic thread, follow figure 2 to wind the thread around points D to G to D eight times, crossing over the marks on the strip of paper.

5. Repeat step 4, working from points E to H to E. It will be necessary to reposition the strip of paper. Then repeat step 4 again, working from points F to J to F.

Figure 1

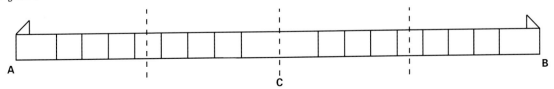

6. Using colored thread, repeat steps 4 and 5, laying the colored threads beside the metallic threads. Finally, remove the strip of paper.

7. To make the wider bands at the outer edges of the pattern, return to the first set of threads between D, G, D, and wind on six rounds of a colored thread. Keep the threads close to each other as you work. The threads will cross over each other at points D and G. Take a few cross-stitches at points D and G to secure the bands.

8. Repeat step 7 at points E, H, E, and then at points F, J, F.

Wrapped Bands 2

For this pattern, you will use three different colors plus a metallic thread. The threads are wrapped around the ball in bands consisting of three rounds of each color followed by two rounds of metallic thread.

MATERIALS

- 3-inch (70-80 mm) ball
- Turquoise polyester sewing thread, 325 yards (300 m)
- Gold metallic thread, 13 yards (12 m)
- Pearl cotton (coton perlé) #5, 1 skein = 27.3 yards (25 m), ¼ skein each of white, red, and medium purple

INSTRUCTIONS

1. Wrap the ball and divide it into 12 vertical sections with a line around the center. Using metallic thread, apply the guidelines.

2. Using the metallic thread you will use for the pattern, stitch around points A and C, stitching under every guideline until there is a 12-sided shape approximately ¾ inch (1.75 cm) across.

3. Since this is a wrapped pattern, you will not be using cut lengths of thread but will be working straight from the skein. Begin by threading a needle directly from the skein of the first color. Enter the wrapped layer with the needle at point 1 on guideline CD as shown in figure 1. Make the needle exit approximately ¾ inch (2 cm) from point 1. Remove the needle, knot the end of the thread, then pull the thread back into the wrapping to hide the knot. Do not pull too hard, or the thread, even with a knot, may pull out of the wrapping.

4. Following figure 1, begin wrapping the first band of the first color starting at point 1 close to point C on guideline CD. Take the thread up past the pin at point G at the centerline. Bring the thread to point 7 close to A; on the other side of the ball, bring the thread down to the pin at point N at the center, then back to point 1 close to C. Note: Point N, which corresponds to point G, is not shown in figure 1 since it is on the other side of the ball.

5. Continue to wrap a second round beside the first. Following figure 1-a, lay the thread to the left of the first round from point 1 to point G; then cross over and lay the thread to the right of the first round from point G to point N; then cross over and lay the thread to the left of the first round from point N to point 1. Note that the crossing over of the threads will always occur at the points around the center.

6. Following step 5 and referring to figure 1-a, lay the thread of the third round next to the second round. Complete four rounds of the first color, then cut the thread from the skein leaving just enough length to fasten off. Working in the same way, wrap two rounds of the metallic thread.

7. Working directly from the skein as in step 3, use the second color of thread to work a similar band starting at point 2 close to point C. Bring the thread to the pin at point H at the center line. Bring the thread to point 8 (on the other side of the ball) close to A; then bring the thread down to the pin at point O at the center, then back to point 2 close to C. Note: Point O, which corresponds to point G, is not shown in figure 1 since it is on the other side of the ball. Wind on four rounds as before, cut the thread from the skein, fasten off, then work two rounds of the metallic thread.

8. Beginning at point 3 close to point C, as you did in steps 3 to 6, work four rounds using the third color of thread followed by two rounds of the metallic thread. When you've completed this band, go back to the first color, continuing to work all subsequent bands in the color sequence 1-2-3 around the ball. When completed, this pattern will have 12 bands.

> **TIP:** *The direction in which you work remains the same for all 12 bands. Note that bands 7 to 12 will cross over the first six bands. Each band must be completed before proceeding to the next. Once all twelve bands are completed, it is difficult to add more rounds.*

Figure 1

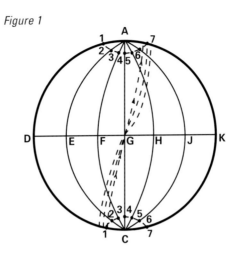

Figure 1-a

3rd round
2nd round
1st round

Wrapped Bands 3

This pattern is similar to Wrapped Bands 2 on page 58 but requires much more thread. Work this pattern on a larger ball for best results. The one shown here was worked on a 3½ inch (85-90 mm) ball. This pattern can be worked exactly the same on a ball with four, six, or eight vertical sections. Just keep in mind that a pattern with eight vertical sections will take considerably more thread than one with four.

MATERIALS

- 3½-inch (85-90 mm) ball
- Yellow polyester sewing thread, 406 yards (375 m)
- Gold metallic thread, 16⅓ yards (15 m)
- Pearl cotton (coton perlé) #5, 1 skein = 27.3 yards (25 m), ⅔ skein each of dark green, medium pink, and coral

INSTRUCTIONS

1. Wrap the ball and divide it into six vertical sections with a line around the center. Use one color of pins for both points A and C, then use a second color of pins for marking all the points around the center. Using metallic thread, apply the guidelines.

2. Following figure 1, use a third color of pins to plot points K, L, M, N, O, and P by placing pins

on each vertical guideline halfway between point A and the center guideline. Note that points K and N will be on guidelines AD and AG. Using the same color of pins, plot points Q, R, S, T, U, and V by placing pins on each vertical guideline halfway between point C and the center guide. Note that points Q and T will be on guidelines CD and CG.

3. Since this is a wrapped pattern, you will not be using cut lengths of thread but will be working straight from the skein. Begin by threading a needle directly from the skein of the first color. Enter the wrapped layer with the needle at point D. Make the needle exit approximately 1¼ inches (3 cm) from point D. Remove the needle, knot one end of the thread, then pull the thread back into the wrapping to hide the knot. Do not pull too hard, or the thread, even with a knot, may pull out of the wrapping.

Figure 1

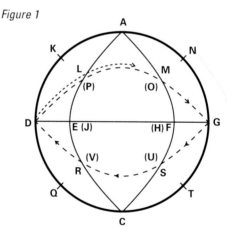

4. Again following figure 1, wind the thread around the ball, passing above the pins at points L and M to G, and then below the pins at points U and V back to D. Note that points U and V are on the other side of the ball.

5. Take the thread around the pin at point D, then, as before, circle the ball, bringing the thread above the pins at points P and O to G, and below the pins at point S and R to D. Note that points O and P are on the other side of the ball.

6. Following steps 4 to 5, complete four rounds in each direction of the first color. As you work, lay the threads in the upper half of the ball above the pins (moving closer to point A); and lay the threads in the lower half of the ball below the pins (moving closer to point C). At points D and G the threads will cross over the threads of the previous rounds. You will need to temporarily secure the thread by winding it around the pin. In the next step you will be changing colors. It is not necessary to fasten off one color before changing, just twist the previous color of thread around the pin until you need it again.

Figure 2

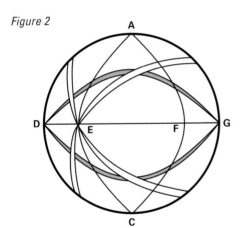

7. Following figure 2, use the second color to repeat steps 3 through 6, beginning at point E, and laying the thread above M and N to H, then below V and Q and back to E. Go around the pin at E and take the thread above K and P to H, and below T and S and back to E, crossing over the centerline at E and H. Work four rounds in each direction.

8. Using the third color, repeat steps 3 through 6, beginning at point F, and laying the thread above

N and O to J, below Q and R and back to F. Go around the pin at F and take the thread above L and K to J, and below U and T and back to F. Work four rounds in each direction.

9. Return to the first color and continue winding the threads in the same order on points D and G, E and H, and F and J, until the wrapping reaches almost to point A at the top and point C at the bottom.

10. Using the same color thread, secure the threads at D, E, F, G, H, and J with two or three stitches. If you prefer, use metallic thread to secure the stitches.

> **TIP:** To help you move easily form point to point as you wrap, you might find it helpful to first write the letters for the points on small pieces of paper, then pin them to the appropriate points.

Patterns around
Four Centers

Plotting Four Centers

Before you begin working with four centers, you need to plot four centers around the ball that are an equal distance from each other. There is no easy way to do this. To help you, I have calculated the positions of these centers based on the various sizes of the balls you will be using.

1. Wrap the ball and divide it into 3, 6, or 12 vertical sections. Using metallic thread, apply the guidelines. A line around the center is *not* required.

2. The top pin at point A will be the center of the first motif. You will plot the second (point D), third (point E), and fourth center (point F), on three of the vertical guidelines AC. Note that unlike the patterns around two centers, point C will no longer be a central point, and you will not be working a motif around it. Use pins of the same color for plotting points A, D, E, and F.

3. The equal distance between each center can be shown in this equation: AD = AE = AF = DE = EF = FD.

4. The calculation for the measurement of line AD is based on the size of ball you are using. To the right are the measurements for the most common ball sizes. Note that the measurement for AD is the same as the diameter of the ball.

5. Once you have determined the distance of line AD, plot points D, E, and F, by placing pins on the guideline as shown in figure 1. It may be necessary to make slight adjustments to points D, E, and F. *Note:* Point F is on the other side of the ball.

Figure 1

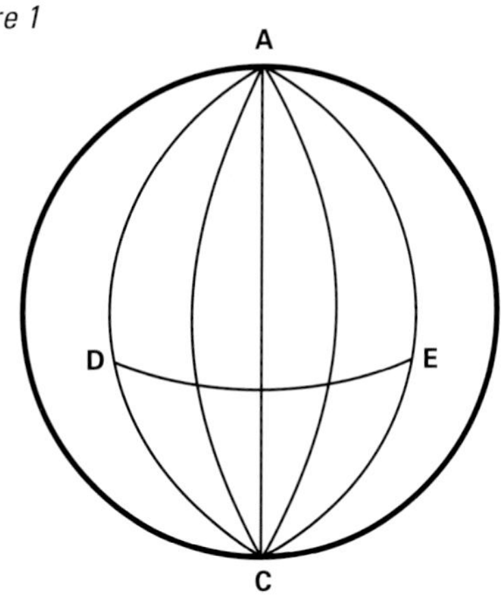

For a ball with a diameter of:

4½ inches (120 mm), AD = 4½ inches (12 cm)

4 inches (100 mm), AD = 4 inches (10 cm)

3½ inches (85-90 mm), AD = 3½ inches (8.5-9 cm)

3 inches (70-80 mm), AD = 3 inches (7-8 cm)

2½ inches (60-65 mm), AD = 2½ inches (6-6.5 cm)

2 inches (50-55 mm), AD = 2 inches (5 cm)

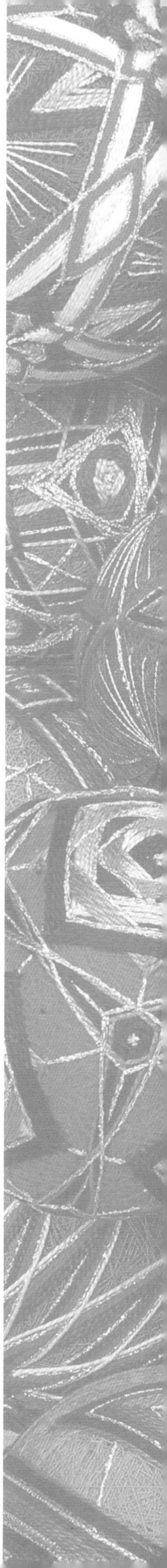

Four Starred Pattern 1

For this pattern, you need to take extra care when plotting the points and placing the pins on the ball. For each different stage of the pattern, use pins of the same color. Since each individual motif is quite small, work in pearl cotton (coton perlé) #8 (coton á broder). For this project I chose four main colors, one for each star, then used two or three shades of that color for each motif. To emphasize the outline of the pattern, finish each motif with a round of metallic thread.

MATERIALS

- 3-inch (70-80 mm) ball
- White polyester sewing thread, 325 yards (300 m)
- Gold metallic thread, 12 yards (11 m)
- Pearl cotton (coton perlé) #8 (coton á broder), 7½ yards (7 m) each of light green, dark green, purple, deep rose, medium blue, dark blue, orange, red, and scarlet

INSTRUCTIONS

1. Wrap the ball and divide it into 12 vertical sections. A line around the center is not required. Using metallic thread, apply the guidelines.

2. Following the general directions for plotting four centers on page 63, and referring to figure 1 on page 63, plot points A, D, E, and F to mark the four centers on the ball. Use blue pins to mark these points. Check that these pins are equidistant from one another; some slight adjustment may be necessary.

3. You will need six guidelines (creating 12 spokes) passing through each of these four points. You do not need to measure these guidelines; you can apply them by eye, since some of the guidelines will pass beside pins already placed on the ball. Once you apply these guidelines, secure the threads at the pin with one or two stitches and fasten off the thread. Continuing to work this way, repeat this step at the blue pins marking the third and fourth centers.

4. You will notice that there are four other points on the ball where six guidelines meet (creating 12 spokes). These points are centrally placed within a triangle created by the four centers in step 3. Place one green pin at each of these points, checking that they are equidistant from one another. Note that point C will be one of these points.

5. Divide the distance between each center pin in half, and mark these points with red pins. These points will be the outer points of the pattern.

6. You will be working with two needles simultaneously. Thread two needles, each with the same color thread. All 12 guidelines need to be worked at the same time—six alternate guidelines with one needle and thread, and the six remaining guidelines between them with the second needle and thread.

7. Following figure 1, plot points around one center (blue pin) by placing pins approximately ⅝ inch (1.75 cm) from the center pin. Work the polystar pattern until the stitching almost reaches the red pin. For an attractive pattern at the center of the star, keep the stitching very close to the center pin. Work as evenly as possible; it is important that the points on the motif be the same length. Work this pattern around all the blue pins. When completed, remove the blue pins.

Figure 1

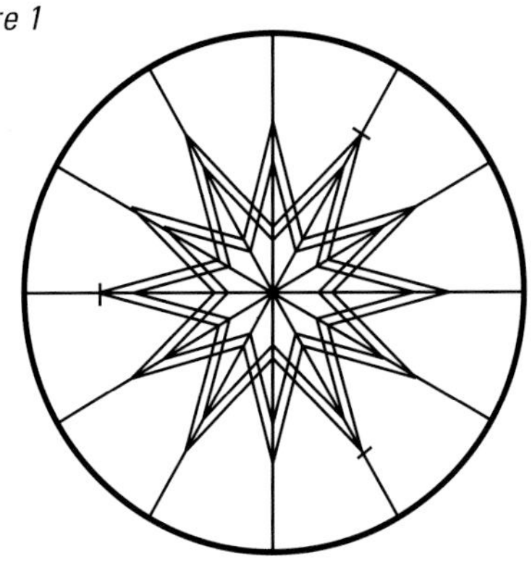

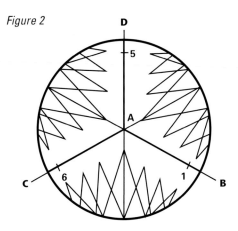

FINISHING THE BALL

To finish, you will work in the spaces between the four motifs. The pattern is centered on the green pins between each polystar pattern and progresses right around the ball. Before you begin, check that the green pins are equidistant from one another; you may need to make slight adjustments. Following figure 2, you may find it helpful to cut out four tiny squares of paper, label them A, B, C, and D, and place one at each green pin. Then, cut out six small squares, number them 1 to 6, and place one at each red pin. As you work the pattern, hold and rotate the ball so that the point where you are stitching always faces toward you.

Figure 2

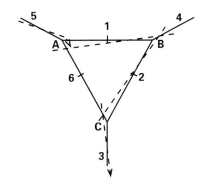

Figure 3

As shown in figure 3, work the pattern as follows:

1. At point A, start to the left of line 6 and go to B, crossing over the line at point 1. Take a stitch from right to left on line 4.

2. Go to point C, crossing over the line at 2, and take a stitch from right to left on line 6.

3. Go to D, crossing over the line at 3, and take a stitch on line 4.

4. Go to A, crossing over the line at 5, and take a stitch on line 6. This brings you back to the starting point.

5. Bring the needle out on line 5 to the left of the line. Go to C, crossing over the line at 6, and take a stitch on line 2.

6. Go to D, crossing over the line at 3, and take a stitch on line 5.

7. Go to B, crossing over the line at 4, and take a stitch on line 2.

8. Go to A, crossing over the line at 1, and take a stitch on line 5. This brings you back to the starting point.

9. Repeat steps 1 to 8 for three or four more rounds to create narrow bands of color between the motifs.

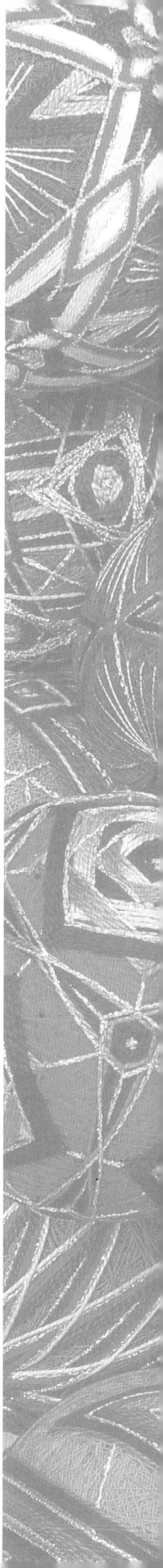

Variation: To create this variation, work the poly-star pattern on six guidelines rather than 12. To make the ball shown you will need: 3-inch (70-80 mm) ball; Pink polyester sewing thread, 325 yards (300 m); Gold metallic thread, 9 yards (8 m); Pearl cotton (coton perlé) #8 (coton á broder); 30 yards (27 m) each of medium blue and dark blue, 15 yards (14 m) each of light green, medium green, and dark green, 7½ yards (7 m) of white.

Wrap the ball and divide it into three vertical sections. A line around the center is not required. Using metallic thread, apply the guidelines. Plot four centers as on page 63. Apply three guidelines creating six spokes at each center.

Follow steps 4 to 7 for the Four Starred Pattern 1 on pages 64 and 65. At step 6, rather than working the polystar pattern on 12 guidelines, work the pattern on six guidelines. Complete the ball by the following steps 1 to 9 for Finishing the Ball on page 65.

Four Starred Pattern 2

The polystar pattern which is worked over the underlying motif creates a star that looks almost three dimensional; using a dark wrapping thread increases this illusion. I worked this pattern on a 4½-inch (120 mm) ball.

MATERIALS
- 4- or 4½-inch (100-120 mm) ball
- Dark green polyester sewing thread, 650 yards (600 m)
- Silver metallic thread, 13 yards (12 m)
- Fine silver metallic thread, 6 yards (5 m)
- Pearl cotton (coton perlé) #5, 1 skein = 27.3 yards (25 m), 1 skein of dark green, ¾ skein each of light green, medium green, white, dark coral, and pink

INSTRUCTIONS
1. Wrap the ball and divide it into 12 vertical sections. Using metallic thread, apply the guidelines. Plot four centers on the ball following the directions on page 63. These points, A, D, E, and F, will be the centers of each motif. Use one color of pin for marking these four points; use a different color of pin for each of the other steps.

2. Each of the center points should have six guidelines crossing at each pin (creating 12 spokes). Apply these additional guidelines.

3. Remove all pins except for those at points A, D, E, and F as before.

4. Following figure 1, plot points G, H, J, K, L, and M by placing pins on the guidelines halfway between each center pin. Plot points O, P, and Q by placing pins on guidelines AF, AD, and AE ½ inch (1.5 cm) from the pin at point A.

Figure 1

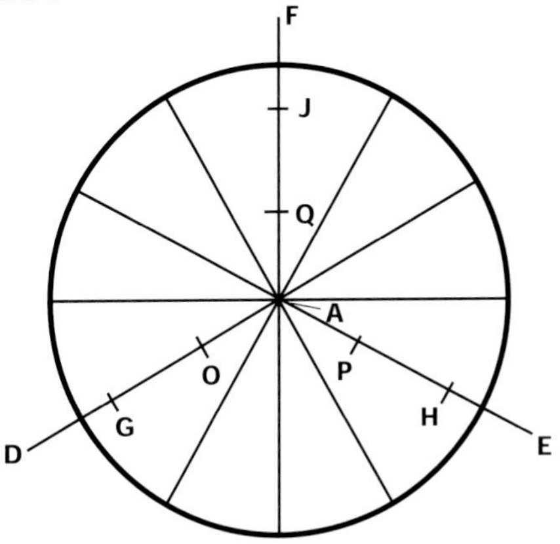

Figure 2

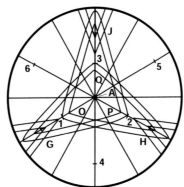

5. Following figure 2, begin working around point A by entering the wrapped layer with the needle and thread so the needle exits below and to the left of the pin at point G. Take a stitch, right to left, at P, then take a stitch at J, take a stitch at O, take a stitch at H, take a stitch at Q, and take a stitch at G. This brings you back to the beginning. Note that it is necessary to stitch twice around the ball to complete a round. As you work around the ball, always stitch from right to left and work around the outside of the pins.

6. Repeat steps 4 and 5 around points D, E, and F. The stitching at each point will overlap the rounds from adjacent patterns.

7. Continue working in this way, changing colors as desired, until the bands of thread are at least ⅜ inch (1 cm) wide around each center.

8. Following figure 2, plot points 1 to 6 for the star pattern around point A. Place pins for points 1, 2, and 3 at the outer edge of the hexagon (at the crossing of the guidelines) approximately 1¼ inches (3 cm) from point A on guidelines AJ, AG, and AH. Place pins for points 4, 5, and 6 approximately 1½ inches (4 cm) from point A on the guidelines in between. Note that points 4, 5, and 6 are also at the crossing points of the guidelines.

9. Work the polystar pattern on these points. The points of the motif will be alternately long and short. Make sure you stitch the center points of the polystar pattern as close to point A as possible. Note that the shorter points will take up the space between the stitching that has already been worked. Lengthen the longer points of the motif with each round so that they almost reach to the next crossing point of the guidelines. Repeat steps 8 and 9 around points D, E, and F.

10. To finish, use the fine metallic thread to work the star motif in each of the remaining four spaces.

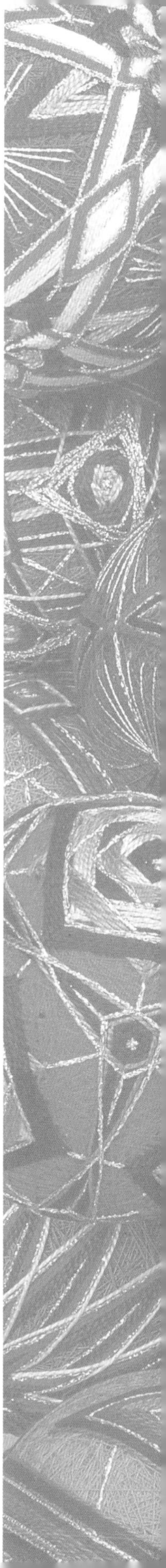

Four Starred Pattern 3

Work this ball in pearl cotton (coton perlé) #8 (coton á broder) to give the pattern a more delicate appearance.

MATERIALS

- 3-inch (70-80 mm) ball
- Dark blue-green polyester sewing thread, 325 yards (300 m)
- Gold metallic thread, 9 yards (8 m)
- Fine gold metallic thread, 4½ yards (4 m)
- Pearl cotton (coton perlé) #8 (coton á broder), 15 yards (14 m) each of white, purple, and medium pink

INSTRUCTIONS

1. Wrap the ball and divide it into six vertical sections. Using metallic thread, apply the guidelines. Plot four centers on the ball following the directions on page 63. These points, A, D, E, and F, will be the centers of each motif. Use one color of pin for marking these four points; use a different color of pin for each of the other steps.

2. You will need three guidelines to cross at each pin (creating six spokes). Apply these additional guidelines.

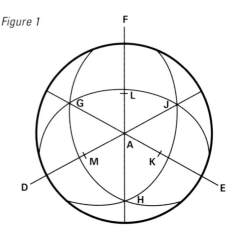

Figure 1

3. Following figure 1, plot points G, H, and J by placing pins where the guidelines cross. Check that these points are all the same distance from A.

4. Following figure 1, plot points K, L, and M around point A by placing the pins approximately 1 inch (2.5 cm) from A. Following figure 2, stitch the polystar pattern from A on AG to M; from M to A on AH; from A on AH to K; from K to A on AJ; from A on AJ to L; from L to A on AG. Work approximately six rounds of the same color.

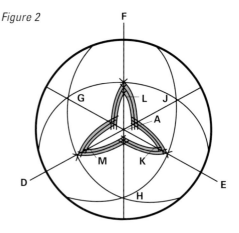

Figure 2

5. Following figure 3, go to the guidelines between those worked in step 4, and work a smaller (shorter) polystar pattern around point A.

6. Repeat steps 4 and 5 around the pins at points D, E, and F.

7. Following figure 4, work a polystar pattern as in steps 4 and 5 at point G. The points of this motif should reach to the points of the star patterns around points A, D, and F. Repeat this step at points H, J, and K.

8. To finish, use the fine metallic thread to work the star motif in the spaces between the pattern motifs.

Figure 3

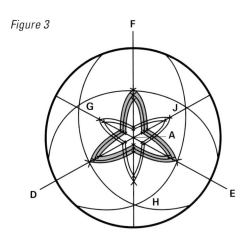

Figure 4

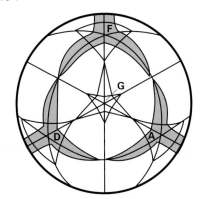

Four Centers Hexagon Pattern 1

Triangles encircle this design to unify the hexagonal motifs. I worked this project on a 4-inch (100 mm) ball which extends the design and exposes more of the wrapping layer. You'll get a much different look if you work it on a smaller ball that will draw the motifs closer together.

MATERIALS
- 4-inch (100 mm) ball
- Light blue polyester sewing thread, 433 yards (400 m)
- Silver metallic thread, 11 yards (10 m)
- Fine silver metallic thread, 4½ yards (4 m)
- Pearl cotton (coton perlé) #5, 1 skein = 27.3 yards (25 m), 1 skein each of red and medium blue, ¾ skein of light blue, ¼ skein of white

INSTRUCTIONS
1. Wrap the ball and divide it into six vertical sections. Using metallic thread, apply the guidelines. Plot four centers on the ball following the directions on page 63. These points, A, D, E, and F, will be the centers of each motif. Use one color of pin for marking these four points; use a different color of pin for each of the other steps.

Figure 1

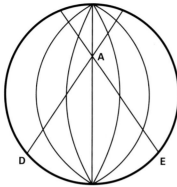

2. As shown in figure 1 you will need three guidelines to cross at each center pin (creating six spokes). Apply these additional guidelines.

3. Following figure 2, plot points G, H, and J by placing pins at the halfway points on guidelines AD, AE, and AF.

Figure 2

4. Again following figure 2, work a small hexagon around the pin at point A by taking stitches on all six spokes. Continue working rounds until the hexagon is approximately ⅜ inch (1 cm) across. Work similar hexagons around points D, E, and F.

5. Return to point A. Again following figure 2, plot points K, L, and M by placing pins on guidelines AD, AE, and AF that are outside the thread of the last round of the hexagon. Make sure these points are equidistant from point A; adjust the pins as necessary.

Figure 3

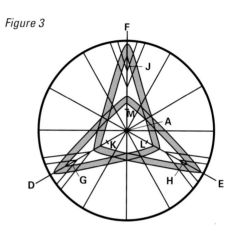

6. Following figure 3, use a different color of thread than you used for the central hexagon, and enter the wrapped layer with the needle and thread so the needle exits to the left of the guideline and just below the pin at point G. Take the thread from point G to point L and take a stitch, right to left. Continuing in this way, work counter clockwise around the ball stitching from L to J to K to H to M to G. Work approximately 12 rounds in this way around point A, changing colors as desired. Then repeat this step around points D, E, and F. The points of *each* motif will overlap the adjacent patterns.

7. Following figure 4, plot points 1, 2, and 3 around point A by placing the pins on the guidelines outside of the thread of the last round of the stitching. Check that each point is equidistant from A. Plot points 4, 5, and 6 on the same guidelines by placing the pins approximately 1½ inch (3.5 cm) from point A.

8. Stitch a few rounds from points 4 to 2, from 2 to 6, from 6 to 1, from 1 to 5, from 5 to 3, and from 3 to 4. Repeat steps 7 and 8 at points D, E, and F.

9. Following figure 5, stitch a triangle by stitching inside points 4, 5, and 6 on each pattern.

10. To finish, use the fine metallic thread to stitch a star motif inside each triangle.

Figure 4

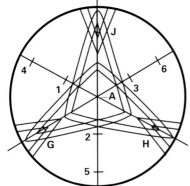

Figure 5

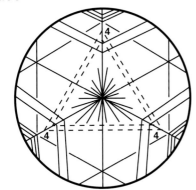

Four Centers Hexagon Pattern 2

Try wrapping a ball in black thread. You'll find it frames the pattern for a handsome presentation of the design.

MATERIALS

- 3-inch (70-80 mm) ball
- Black polyester sewing thread, 325 yards (300 m)
- Gold metallic thread, 11 yards (10 m)
- Pearl cotton (coton perlé) #5, 1 skein = 27.3 yards (25 m), ¾ skein each of white and light blue, ½ skein of red

INSTRUCTIONS

1. Wrap the ball and divide it into six vertical sections. Using metallic thread, apply the guidelines. Plot four centers on the ball following the directions on page 63. These points, A, D, E, and F, will be the centers of each motif. Use one color of pin for marking these four points; use a different color of pin for each of the other steps.

2. You will need three guidelines to cross at each pin (creating six spokes). Apply these additional guidelines.

3. Following figure 1, plot points G, H, and J by placing pins where the guidelines cross. For marking these points, use pins of a different color than those used in step 1. Check that these pins are equidistant from A.

4. Following figure 2, stitch two rounds of a hexagon around point A, beginning the hexagon as close to A as possible.

5. Again following figure 2, plot points K, L, M, N, O, and P by placing pins approximately 1 inch (2.5 cm) from point A on each of the guidelines.

Figure 1

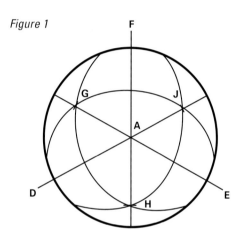

6. Change thread color and stitch a triangle around A, stitching from K to M to O to K. Always hold the ball so that the point where you are stitching is toward you, and work the stitch from right to left. Stitch three rounds.

7. Change thread color and work three more rounds from L to N to P to L.

8. Continue stitching triangles around point A in this way, as in steps 6 and 7, changing colors as desired, until the stitching reaches almost to points G, H, and J. Note that each triangle will overlap the previous one.

9. Work similar triangles around points D, E, and F.

10. Complete the ball by following steps 1 to 9 for Finishing the Ball on page 65.

Four Centers Hexagon Pattern 3

The bands around the hexagons create a delicate tracery around the ball. The space between motifs is increased by using pearl cotton (coton perlé) #8 (coton á broder).

MATERIALS
- 3-inch (70-80 mm) ball
- White polyester sewing thread, 325 yards (300 m)
- Gold metallic thread, 9 yards (8 m)
- Fine gold metallic thread, 4½ yards (4 m)
- Pearl cotton (coton perlé) #8 (coton á broder), 15 yards (14 m) each of green, light blue, and purple

Figure 2

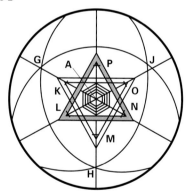

Figure 1

INSTRUCTIONS

1. Wrap the ball and divide it into six vertical sections. Using metallic thread, apply the guidelines. Plot four centers on the ball following the directions on page 63. These points, A, D, E, and F, will be the centers of each motif. Use one color of pin for marking these four points; use a different color of pin for each of the other steps.

2. As shown in figure 1, you will need three guidelines to cross at each pin (creating six spokes). Apply these additional guidelines. Remove all the pins except the pins at points A, D, E, and F.

3. Using one color, stitch a hexagon of approximately eight rounds around point A.

4. Following figure 1, plot points G, H, J, K, L, and M by placing pins halfway between each center pin on the guidelines. Note that points K, L, and M are not shown since they are on the other side of the ball. Plot points O, P, and Q by placing pins approximately ½ inch (1.5 cm) from point A on guidelines AG, AH and AJ. The pins should be at the edges of the hexagon.

5. Again following figure 1, enter the wrapped layer with the needle and thread so the needle exits to the left of the guideline just below pin G. Take the thread to P and take a stitch, right to left.

Then take a stitch at J; take a stitch at O; take a stitch at H, take a stich at Q, then at G. This brings you back to the beginning. You will need to stitch twice around the ball to complete a round. Always stitch from right to left, stitching outside the pins. Repeat this step.

6. Repeat steps 3, 4, and 5 around points D, E, and F. Note that the stitching at points G, H, and J will overlap the adjacent patterns.

7. Continue working in this way, as in step 5, changing colors as desired, until the bands of thread around each center point are at least ⅜ inch (1 cm) wide.

Figure 2

8. Following figure 2, plot points 1 to 6 around point A by placing pins 1, 2, and 3 at the outer points of the hexagon, then placing pins 4, 5, and 6 approximately 1½ inches (4 cm) from A on the same guidelines as points 1, 2, and 3.

9. Stitch from point 1 to point 5, 5 to 3, 3 to 4, 4 to 2, 2 to 6, and 6 to 1. Continuing in this way, work a few rounds. Then repeat steps 8 and 9 around points D, E, and F.

10. To finish, use the fine metallic thread to work a star motif at the four points where the stitching meets at points 4, 5, and 6.

Patterns Around

Six Centers

Square Pattern 1

Plotting the points for six centers is very easy.
All you need is point A at the top, point C at the
bottom, and four equally spaced points around
the center of the ball.

MATERIALS

- 3-inch (70-75 mm) ball
- Turquoise polyester sewing thread,
  325 yards (300 m)
- Silver metallic thread, 12 yards (10 m)
- Fine silver metallic thread, 9 yards (8 m)
- Pearl cotton (coton perlé) #5, 1 skein = 27.3 yards
  (25 m), 1 skein each of white, red and purple

INSTRUCTIONS

1. Wrap the ball and divide it into eight vertical
sections with a line around the center. Note that
the pins at points A, C, D, E, F, and G will
become the six centers of the design.

2. Using metallic thread, apply the guidelines.
Add two more guidelines at four pins around the
center, following the instructions on page 12, to
give you four lines at each pin (creating eight
spokes). See figure 1.

3. Following figure 2, use the paper measuring
strip to plot points H, J, K, and L by placing
pins halfway between point A and the centerline
on guidelines AD, AE, AF, and AG. Note that
these points will become the outer corners of the
first square.

Figure 1

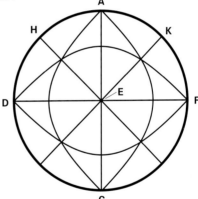

Figure 2

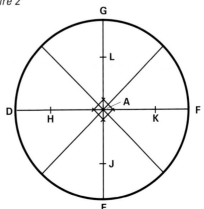

4. Again following figure 2, begin stitching a square around point A. To do this, enter the wrapped layer with the needle and thread so the needle exits close to point A and just to the left of guideline AD. Working counterclockwise around the ball, take a stitch, right to left, close to A on guideline AE, then take a stitch on AF, then take a stitch on AG, then back to AD. This completes one round.

5. Work as many rounds as needed to make a square whose outer corners reach points H, J, K, and L. Vary your colors by working rounds in different colors. Take care to keep your work as even as possible. You want the shape to be exactly square so it will meet the other squares at their four corners. Measure your work from time to time to check that the corners of the square are proceeding along all four guidelines from point A at the same rate.

6. When you complete the first square, fasten off the thread and repeat steps 3 through 5 around another center on the ball. Repeat all the squares in exactly the same way until you have six separate squares centered around the points A, C, D, E, F, and G.

Figure 3

7. When all six squares are complete, each corner should touch the corner of the neighboring squares, leaving triangular spaces between the squares. Following figure 3, finish the design by working the star motif in the triangular spaces.

> **TIP:** *Each square can be worked in identical colors. If desired, all six squares can be worked simultaneously. To do this, work the first set of rounds in the first color around each point, then change colors to work the second set of rounds in the second color around each point. Continue in this way until the squares are complete.*

Square Pattern 2

The illusion of intertwining squares is made by working the motif so that one square overlaps another around the ball. A few rounds of the first color can be worked before changing colors. Work this pattern on a 2- or 2½-inch (50-65 mm) ball using #8 pearl cotton (coton á broder). Since the sides of the square are longer than the pattern on page 75 (previous), using a larger ball and thicker thread would prevent the threads from lying close together.

MATERIALS

- 2- or 2½-inch (50-65 mm) ball
- Red polyester sewing thread, 190 yards (175 m)
- Gold metallic thread, 6 yards (5 m)
- Fine gold thread, 6 yards (5 m)
- Pearl cotton (coton perlé) #8 (coton á broder), 15 yards (14 m) each of white, light blue, and medium blue

INSTRUCTIONS

1. Wrap the ball and divide it into eight vertical sections with a line around the center.

2. Using metallic thread, apply the guidelines. Add two more guidelines at four pins around the center, following the instructions on page 12, to give you four lines at each pin (creating eight spokes). See figure 1 on page 75.

3. Following figure 1 below, plot points H, J, K, and L by placing pins halfway between point A and the centerline on guidelines AD, AE, AF, and AG.

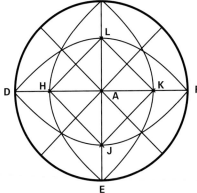

Figure 1

4. Again following figure 1, begin stitching at point H by entering the wrapped layer with the needle and thread so the needle exits below the pin at point H and just to the left of guideline AD. Since you will be forming the square outside

of the points, take a stitch right to left below the pin at point J. Continue in this way, working counterclockwise around the ball, taking a stitch below K, taking a stitch below L, then back to H. Work two or three rounds.

5. Following figure 2, and working below the pins as you did in step 4, move to point G and work a square around L, M, N, and O. Note that the squares will overlap at one corner. Work the same number of rounds as in step 4.

Figure 2

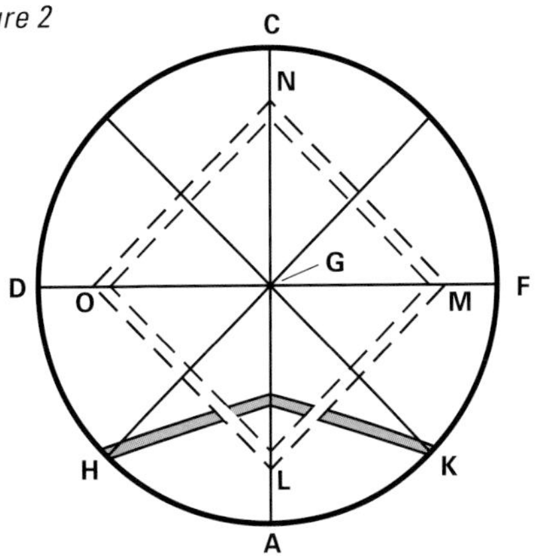

6. Continue working in this way around the ball until you've worked four square bands of color centered on points A, G, C, and E, with each square having the same number of rounds.

7. As you did in steps 3 to 5, work two more squares centered on points D and F. Remove all pins.

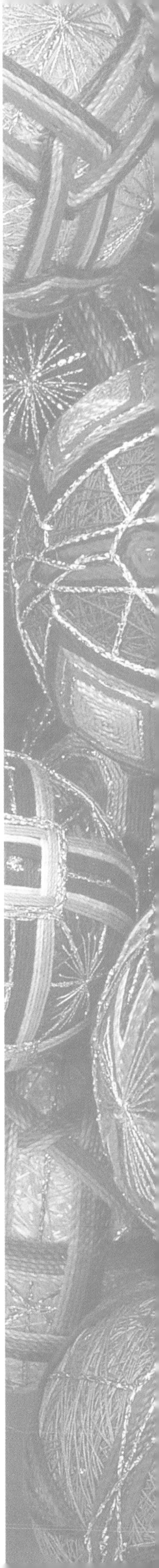

8. Go back to point A. As you did in steps 3 through 7, work a few rounds of a different color. Then do the same on the squares centered on points G, C, E, D, and F. When completed, work the same way with another color, then continue in this way until you've completed your chosen color sequence. Note: You must work all the squares in the same order as in steps 3 to 7. If you don't, the corners of the squares will not overlap in the same way. To help you keep track of the sequence, pin pieces of paper, numbered 1 to 6, to the center of each square.

9. When you've completed all six squares, finish the ball by working the star motif in the center of each square.

Variation: Work only four squares, centered on points A, G, C, and E. Decorate points D and F with a star motif. Then work a small square or star in the center of each of the worked squares at points A, G, C, and E.

Square Pattern 3

The combination of Square Pattern 2 worked at four points around the center of the ball and the Square Crossing Pattern worked at the top and bottom, creates an interesting overlapped design with six centers. Work this pattern on a smaller, 2- or 2½-inch (50-65 mm) ball.

MATERIALS

- 2- or 2½-inch (50-65 mm) ball
- Dark blue polyester sewing thread, 190 yards (175 m)
- Gold metallic thread, 6 yards (5 m)
- Pearl cotton (coton perlé) #8 (coton á broder), 15 yards (14 m) each of light purple, pink, and white

INSTRUCTIONS

1. Wrap the ball and divide it into eight vertical sections with a line around the center.

2. Using metallic thread, apply the guidelines. Add two more guidelines at four pins around the center, following the instructions on page 12, to give you four lines at each pin (creating eight spokes).

3. Following figure 1, which shows the top of the ball, plot points H, J, K, and L by placing pins halfway between point A and the centerline on guidelines AD, AE, AF, and AG.

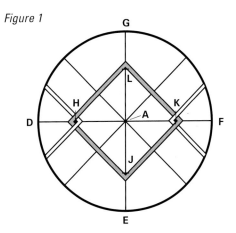

Figure 1

4. Again following figure 1, stitch a square around the outside of pins H, J, K, and L. Point A will be the center of the square. Stitch six or seven rounds in your choice of colors.

5. As you did in steps 3 and 4, stitch squares with points C, D, and F as the center points.

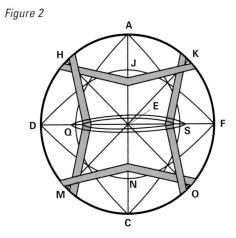

Figure 2

6. To finish off the top and bottom of the ball, follow figure 2. Thread two needles with the same color thread. Take a stitch at point Q, then lay the thread to the right of, and next to, guideline SEQ. Turn the ball so that point S is toward you, and take a stitch from right to left at S, then lay the thread to the right of line SEQ. Work four to five rounds. Using the second needle, repeat on lines NEJ, working the same number of rounds as worked on SEQ.

7. Repeat step 6 on the other side of the ball on lines RGT, then LGP.

8. Change thread colors and repeat steps 6 and 7. Continue in this way until the stitching overlaps halfway into the squares already stitched. You can vary the number of rounds and, therefore, the colors as desired.

9. Stitch squares around the pins at points A, D, C, and F. These will be at centers of the squares worked in steps 4 and 5.

Square Pattern 4

With small squares on each of the six centers, this design provides enough space in between for working a double ring of polystars around the ball.

MATERIALS
- 3-inch ball
- Pale blue polyester sewing thread, 325 yards (300 m)
- Silver metallic thread, 9 yards (8 m)
- Pearl cotton (coton perlé) #5, 1 skein = 27.3 yards (25 m), ⅓ skein red, ½ skein each of turquoise, royal blue, dark blue, maroon

INSTRUCTIONS

1. Wrap the ball and divide it into eight vertical sections with a line around the center. Note that the pins at points A, C, D, E, F, and G will become the six centers of the design.

2. Using metallic thread, apply the guidelines. Add two more guidelines at four pins around the center, following the instructions on page 12, to give you four additional lines at each pin (creating eight spokes).

3. Following figure 1, plot points S, T, U, and V by placing pins at the crossing point of the guidelines as shown. Check that the pins are equidistant from point A.

4. Following figure 2, begin stitching a square around point A. To do this, enter the wrapped layer with the needle and thread so the needle exits close to point A and just to the left of guideline AD. Working counterclockwise around the ball, take a stitch, right to left, close to A on guideline AE, then take a stitch on AF, then take a stitch on AG, then back to AD. This completes one round. Work enough rounds, changing colors as desired, to make a square approximately 1 inch (2.5 cm) square.

5. Work squares as above around points G, E, C, D, and F. As shown in the photograph, you want the distance between the corners of the squares to equal the length of the sides of the squares. To do this, you will need to work as evenly as possible. You may find it helpful to work all squares simultaneously, alternating rounds around each point. This will keep your work even and will ensure that the squares are uniform in size.

6. When you've completed the squares, begin working a polystar pattern (see page 17) around the pin at point S, as shown in figure 3. Continue working the polystar pattern until the points of one band of stitching reach the sides of the squares already worked.

Figure 1

7. Work another set of rounds of the polystar pattern between the points of the first rounds until the points reach the guidelines between the squares.

Figure 2

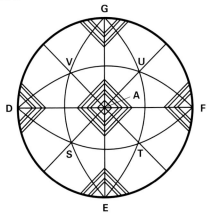

Figure 3

TIP: *Since you will be working the polystar pattern on only six guidelines, try to keep the points as deep as possible. Be aware that the line between the points of the pattern can become almost a straight line. This will prevent the threads from lying flat, particularly at the top stitch.*

Variation on
Square Pattern 4

Similar to the preceding pattern, Square Pattern 4, this design has larger squares with hexagonal tristars worked in between.

MATERIALS
- 3-inch (70-75 mm) ball
- Dark jade green polyester sewing thread, 325 yards (300 m)
- Gold metallic thread, 13 yards (12 m)
- Pearl cotton (coton perlé) #5, 1 skein = 27.3 yards (25 m), 1 skein of red, ¾ skein of navy blue, ½ skein each of medium blue and light blue

INSTRUCTIONS
1. Following figure 1, complete steps 1 through 5 as for Square Pattern 4 on page 80, working the squares until there is a distance of approximately ½ inch (1.5 cm) between the corners of each square pattern. Once you plot points S, T, U, and V, and W, X, Y, and Z on the other side of the ball, you may find it helpful to pin small squares of paper with S, T, U, and V written on them to their corresponding points to guide you as you work.

2. Following figure 2, turn the ball so point S is facing you. Plot points 1, 2, and 3 by placing pins halfway between points S and T, S and V, and S and W.

3. Again following figure 2, begin stitching close to point S by entering the wrapped layer with the needle and thread so the needle exits close to point S and to the left of guideline ST. Take a stitch from right to left at point 1 on guideline SV. Take a stitch close to S on SW. Take a stitch at 2 on ST. Take a stitch close to S on SV. Take a stitch at 3 on SW. Take a stitch close to S on ST. Continue stitching around point S in this way until you have worked four or five rounds.

4. Repeat step 3 around points T, U, V, W, X, Y, and Z. The points of each pattern should overlap the points of the next. Note that points W, X, Y, and Z, which correspond to points S, T, U, and V, are not shown in figure 1, since they are on the other side of the ball.

Figure 1

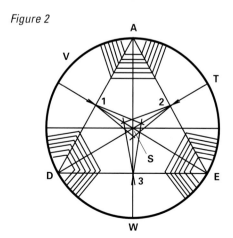

Figure 2

Variation on

The Square Pattern

Though this may look like a series of diamonds, the pattern is a variation of the intertwining squares worked in Square Pattern 2 on page 76. Work this pattern on a smaller 2- or 2½-inch (50-65 mm) ball.

MATERIALS

- 2- or 2½-inch (50-65 mm) ball
- Light blue polyester sewing thread, 217 yards (200 m)
- Gold metallic thread, 3 yards (2.5 m)
- Pearl cotton (coton perlé) #5, 1 skein = 27.3 yards (25 m), ½ skein each of medium blue and dark blue

INSTRUCTIONS

1. Wrap the ball and divide it into 16 vertical divisions with a line around the center. Using metallic thread, apply the guidelines.

2. Following figure 1, plot points 1, 3, 5, and 7 by placing pins ¾ inch (2 cm) from point A on alternate guidelines. Plot points 2, 4, 6, and 8 by placing pins ¾ inch (2 cm) from point C on the same alternate guidelines as points 1, 3, 5, and 7.

3. Again following figure 1, stitch a square around pins 1, D, 2, and F, working the around the outside of each pin.

4. Continue working rounds outside of each pin until the corners of the squares meet the guidelines at points R and G. Note that point R, which is next to point D, is not shown in the diagram since it is on the other side of the ball.

5. Stitch a second square around pins 3, F, 4, and H until the corners of the squares meet the guidelines at points E and J.

6. Repeat steps 3 and 4 around the ball until all eight squares have been completed. Note that where one square crosses another, it should be alternately woven over and under the previous squares.

Figure 1

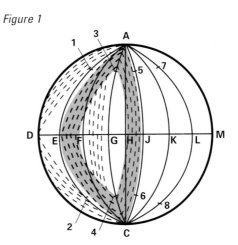

Square Pattern 7

Borrowing the hexagonal pattern from the Four Starred Pattern on page 65 provides a starry complement to the square motifs.

MATERIALS

Red Ball

- 3-inch (70-80 mm) ball
- Red polyester sewing thread, 325 yards (300 m)
- Gold metallic thread, 11 yards (10 m)
- Pearl cotton (coton perlé) #5, 1 skein = 27.3 yards (25 m), 1 skein each of light blue, dark blue, and blue-gray, ¼ skein of purple

Turquoise Ball

- 3-inch (70-80 mm) ball
- Turquoise polyester sewing thread, 325 yards (300 m)
- Silver metallic thread, 11 yards (10 m)
- Fine silver metallic thread, 9 yards (8 m)
- Pearl cotton (coton perlé) #5, 1 skein = 27.3 yards (25 m), 1 skein each of white, red, and purple

INSTRUCTIONS

1. Wrap the ball and divide it into eight vertical sections with a line around the center. Note that the pins at points A, C, D, E, F, and G will become the six centers of the design.

2. Using metallic thread, apply the guidelines. Add two more guidelines at points D, E, F, and G, following the instructions on page 12, to give you four lines at each pin (creating eight spokes).

3. Following figure 1, plot points H, J, K, and L by placing pins halfway between point A and the centerline on guidelines AD, AE, AF, and AG. Note that these points will become the outer corners of the square pattern.

4. Following figure 2, begin stitching a square around point A. To do this, enter the wrapped layer with the needle and thread so the needle exits close to point A and just to the left of guideline AD. Working counterclockwise around the ball, take a stitch, right to left, close to A on guideline AE, then take a stitch on AF, then take a stitch on AG, then back to AD. This completes one round. Work four or five rounds.

Figure 1

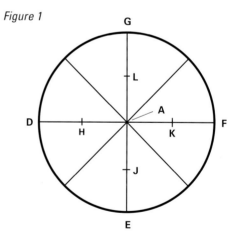

5. Again following figure 2, change the thread color and stitch the same number of rounds on the guidelines between those already worked. Note that these rounds will overlap the previous rounds.

6. Return to the first set of guidelines. Repeat steps 4 and 5 until the stitching almost reaches points H, J, K, and L.

7. Repeat steps 4 through 6 around points C, D, E, F and G.

8. When you complete the square motifs, note the eight triangular spaces left between the squares. Place a pin at the center of each of these spaces where the guidelines cross. Check that the pins are the same distance from each other. Following steps 1 through 9 for Finishing the Ball on page 65, work the hexagonal pattern around the ball.

Figure 2

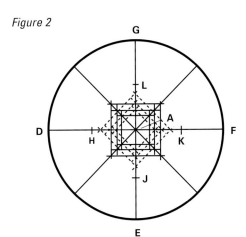

Variation: To finish the ball in a different way, do not work step 8; instead use fine metallic thread to work the star motif in the triangular spaces.

Hexagonals on Six Centers

This pattern has six centers, allowing you to work the hexagonal motif around each central point. The project shown here is stitched on a 2½-inch (65 mm) diameter ball.

MATERIALS

- 2- or 2½-inch (50-65 mm) ball
- Medium blue polyester sewing thread, 275 yards (250 m)
- Gold metallic thread, 9 yards (8 m)
- Fine gold metallic thread, 6¼ yards (6 m)
- Pearl cotton (coton perlé) #5, 1 skein = 27.3 yards (25 m), ½ skein each of light blue, deep rose, and maroon

INSTRUCTIONS

1. Wrap and divide the ball into eight vertical sections with a line around the center. Using metallic thread, apply the guidelines. For this pattern, you will also need four lines (eight spokes) at each of the six centers. To plot this, follow the instructions for Plotting Points for Patterns with Multiple Centers on page 12.

2. Following figure 1, stitch a triangle around the pins at points ADF. To do this, enter the wrapped layer with the needle and thread so the needle exits just to the left of the guideline AJ at point A. Take the thread down to point D, and take a

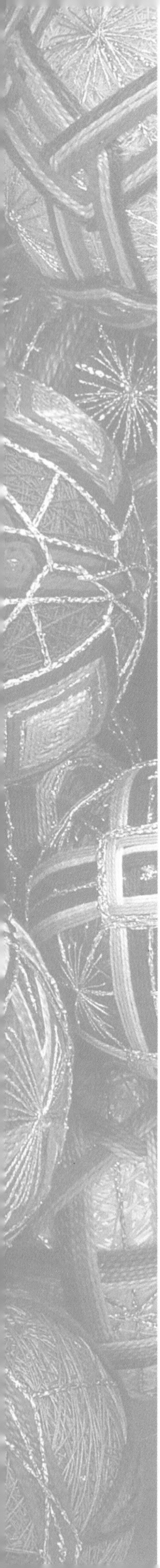

Figure 1

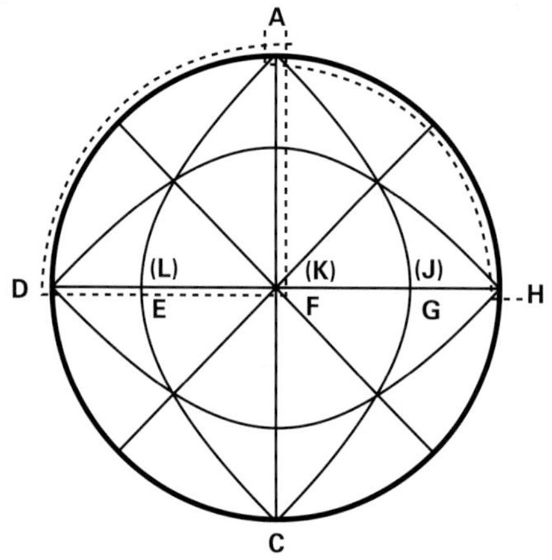

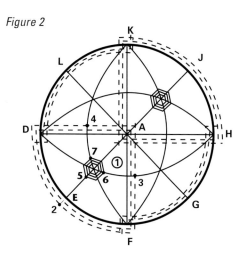

Figure 2

4. Return to the first triangle made on points ADF and stitch another round. Then stitch another round at the other three triangles made on points AHK, FCH, and KDC. Working the triangles in this sequence, complete six rounds.

5. Following figure 2, place pins at the center of each of the four triangles where the six guidelines cross. Using the strip of paper you made for dividing the ball, check that the pins are equally spaced from the three corners of the triangles. Stitch a hexagon around each of these pins by taking a stitch on each guideline at the pin. Work six rounds to complete the hexagon.

6. Note that figure 2 shows you where hexagon 1 is positioned in relation to the ball, while figure 3 is an enlarged detail of hexagon 1. Referring to figures 2 and 3, begin with hexagon 1 and plot points 2, 3, and 4 by placing pins on the outer side of triangle ADF. Plot points 5, 6, and 7 on the same lines by placing the pins at the edge of the hexagon.

7. Following figure 3, stitch from point 2 to point 6, from 6 to 4, from 4 to 5, from 5 to 3, from 3 to 7, and from 7 to 2. This completes one round. Work six rounds.

stitch right to left on the outer side of the pin on the guideline between DC and DK. Take the thread to point F, and take a stitch at the outer side of the pin on the guideline between FC and FH. Then return to point A, entering the wrapped layer just right of guideline AJ. In the same way, stitch a second triangle around the pins at points AHK. Note that these two triangles will overlap at point A.

3. As you did in step 2, stitch triangles around the pins at points FCH and KDC. Note that the points of each triangle will overlap the point of another's.

Figure 3

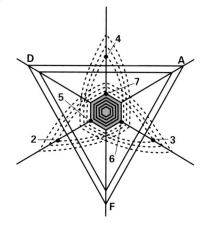

8. Repeat steps 6 and 7 in each of the triangles. Note that the points at 2, 3, and 4 should meet in the centers of the triangular spaces left between the stitched triangles.

9. Stitch a star motif at the meeting points of the pattern at points 2, 3, and 4.

> **TIP:** *It will help if you write the letters A, C, D, E, F, G, H, J, K, and L on small pieces of paper and pin each one on the ball at the appropriate position.*

Six Star Pattern

Since the motifs are small, they could be worked in pearl cotton (coton perlé) #8 (coton á broder). I worked the six stars with pearl cotton (coton perlé) #5 in two blues and white; then for the last round of the pattern, I used metallic thread.

MATERIALS

- 3-inch (70-75 mm) ball
- Red polyester sewing thread, 325 yards (300 m)
- Gold metallic thread, 11 yards (10 m)
- Fine gold metallic thread, 9 yards (8 m)
- Pearl cotton (coton perlé) #5, 1 skein = 27.3 yards (25 m), 1 skein each in white, light blue, and medium blue

INSTRUCTIONS

1. Wrap the ball and divide it into eight vertical sections with a line around the center.

2. Using metallic thread, apply the guidelines. Add two more guidelines at the four pins around the center, following the instructions on page 12, to give you four lines at each pin (creating eight spokes).

3. Following figure 1, plot points H, J, K, and L by placing pins approximately ¾ inch (2 cm) from point A.

4. Work the polystar pattern (see page 17) around point A. Begin stitching close to the pin at point A on guideline AD. Take a stitch at point H, take a stitch close to point A on AE. Take a stitch at J. Continue working this way counterclockwise around the ball until you are back to point A on guideline AD. Work several rounds.

5. Work the polystar pattern around each of the remaining five centers C, D, E, F, and G. The outer points of each star should almost touch the points of the next pattern. You may need to work additional rounds on each motif until the points nearly meet. Remove the pins from points H, J, K, and L.

Figure 1

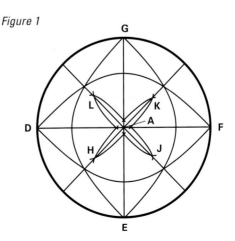

6. Return to the first motif worked around point A. Following figure 2, plot points M, N, O, and P by placing pins halfway between point A and the centerline on guidelines AD, AE, AF, and AG.

7. Again following figure 2, stitch on the points plotted in step 6. Begin close to point A on line AH. Take a stitch at point N. Take a stitch close to point A on line AJ. Take a stitch at O. Take a stitch close to A on line AK. Take a stitch at P. Take a stitch close to point A on AL. Take a stitch at M. This completes one round. Work four or five rounds.

8. Repeat step 7 around points C, C, E, F, and G. Note that each of the points of the motifs will overlap the points of the next motif.

9. To finish, work the star motif in the spaces between the points of the stars.

Figure 2

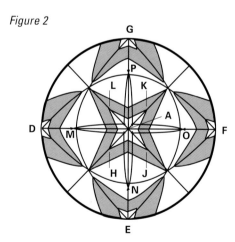

Six Star Pattern 2

The pattern uses four overlapping triangles worked around the ball, and a repeated hexagonal tristar motif to create this striking design.

MATERIALS

- 3-inch (70-80 mm) ball
- Light blue polyester sewing thread, 325 yards (300 m)
- Gold metallic thread, 11 yards (10 m)
- Pearl cotton (coton perlé) #5, 1 skein = 27.3 yards (25 m), 1 skein each of purple and emerald green, 3/4 skein each of dark red and medium green.

INSTRUCTIONS

1. Wrap and divide the ball into eight vertical sections with a line around the center.

2. Using metallic thread, apply the guidelines. Add two more guidelines at the four pins, D, E, F, and G around the centerline, following the instructions on page 12, to give you four lines at each pin (creating eight spokes).

3. Following figure 1, work around the pins at points A, E, and F first to stitch a triangle outside of the pins. Take care to stitch under the center guideline at each point.

Figure 1

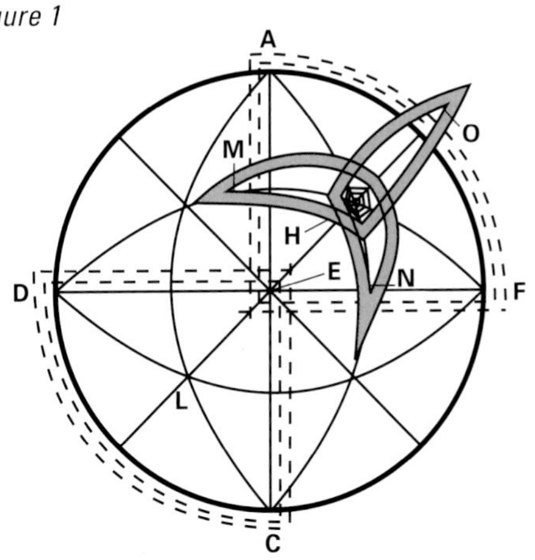

4. When the rounds of the triangle are a few threads wide, turn the ball and work a triangle around pins A, G, and D.

5. As you did in steps 3 and 4, work triangles around points C, F, and G, and C, D, and E.

6. Return to the first triangle around points A, E, and F made in step 3, and work some rounds in another color. Then repeat these same colors around the other triangles in order, working around A, G, and D, then C, F, and G, then C, D, and E.

7. Plot points H, J, K, and L by placing pins where the guidelines cross at the center of each of the four triangles. Use the paper measuring strip to check that these points are accurately placed. Note that points J and K are on the other side of the ball.

8. Following figure 1, begin working around point H to stitch a hexagon of six rounds. Plot points M, N, and O by placing pins outside of the threads of the triangle, positioning them halfway between the corners of the triangle.

9. Work the hexagonal tristar pattern as you did for Hexagonal Tristar 1 on page 47, stitching from point M to close to H on HN; from H on HN to O; from O close to H on HM; from H on HM to N; from N to close to H on HO; and from H on HO to M. Continuing this way, work a few rounds until the points at M, N, and O reach to the center of the triangles.

10. Repeat step 9 around points J, K, and L. The points of these patterns should all meet where the guidelines cross at the center of each of the four triangles left between the stitched triangles. Work a hexagon for a few rounds around the outside of each hexagonal tristar pattern.

11. To finish, if desired, a star motif could be worked between the points of the hexagonal tristars.

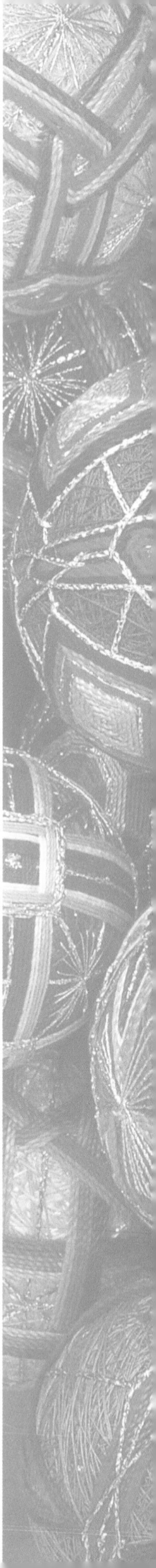

Lace Star

As you work the herringbone stitch around the points of the ball, you can see that this pattern is a distant cousin to the polystars. The spaced stitching gives this design its delicate, lacy appearance, and will look best when worked in only one color.

MATERIALS

- 3-inch (70-75 mm) ball
- White polyester sewing thread, 325 yards (300 m)
- Silver metallic thread, 5 yards (4 m)
- Pearl cotton (coton perlé) #5, 1 skein = 27.3 yards (25 m), 1 skein of blue

INSTRUCTIONS

1. Wrap the ball and divide it into 16 vertical sections with a line around the center. Using metallic thread, apply the guidelines. You will need eight guidelines at each center. To do this, use the metallic thread to apply six more guidelines at each pin around the center to give you eight lines (creating 16 spokes) at each of the six centers.

2. Enter the wrapped layer with the needle and thread so the needle exits close to point A and to the left of guideline AE. Working counterclockwise around the ball, work the herringbone stitch, right to left, on every other guideline as you did for the polystar patterns. At this stage,

you should be able to measure the depth of the stitches by eye. Work one round.

3. Work one round as you did in step 2 on the guidelines in between those already worked. Keep the top stitches as close to point A as possible, but make the bottom stitches lower than in the first round. This round will overlap the first round worked on the other set of guidelines.

4. Following figure 1, work a third round on the same guidelines as in step 2. This round will overlap the round made in step 3.

Figure 1

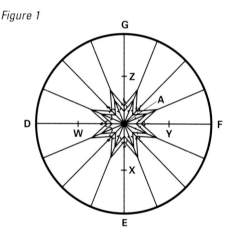

5. At this point, to make sure the stitching progresses evenly, plot points on alternate guidelines that are approximately 1 inch (2.5 cm) from point A to check that the stitching is kept even.

6. Continue to work this way on alternate guidelines for every round so the rounds continue to overlap. For a more pronounced effect that creates a thicker band, stitch two rounds before changing to the next set of guidelines. From time to time, check that the points of the pattern are all equidistant from A. Work until the pattern is almost to the points W, X, Y, and Z. Note that these points are plotted halfway between A and D, A and E, A and F, and A and G. The photo shows three single rounds followed by two double rounds of thread.

7. Repeat steps 2 through 6 around points C, D, E, F, and G.

8. You can decorate each space between the six lacy motifs with a small star motif.

Octagonal Star

By using pearl cotton (coton perlé) #8 (coton á broder) on a 3-inch (70-80 mm) ball, you expose more of the wrapped layer, which allows the pattern thread to create a delicate tracery around the central octagons.

MATERIALS

- 3-inch (70-80 mm) ball
- Medium blue polyester sewing thread, 325 yards (300 m)
- Silver metallic thread, 11 yards (10 m)
- Pearl cotton (coton perlé) #8 (coton á broder), 15 yards (14 m) each of red, light turquoise, and purple

INSTRUCTIONS

1. Wrap and divide the ball into eight vertical sections with a line around the center.

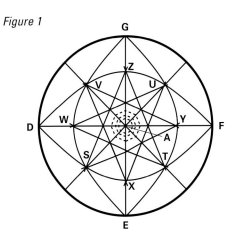

Figure 1

2. Using metallic thread, apply the guidelines. Add two more guidelines at four pins around the center, following the instructions on page 12, to give you four lines at each pin (creating eight spokes).

3. Following figure 1, begin as close to point A as possible and stitch an octagon around point A. Work a few rounds in the first color, then change to another color, continuing to stitch rounds until the octagon is at least ½ inch (1.5 cm) from point A.

4. Plot points W, X, Y, and Z by placing pins where two guidelines cross. These points should be halfway between A and D, A and E, A and F, and A and G.

5. In the same way, plot points S, T, U, and V on the guidelines in between the guidelines in step 4. These points should be the same distance from A as points W, X, Y, and Z.

6. Again following figure 1, enter the wrapped layer with the needle and thread so the needle exits just below the pin at point S and to the left of the guideline. Take the thread to Y and take a stitch, right to left. Work counter clockwise around the ball to take a stitch at V, take a stitch at X, take a stitch at U, take a stitch at W, take a stitch at T, take a stitch at Z, and take a stitch at S.

Work two or three rounds in this way. The photo shows one round in silver, followed by one round of red.

7. Repeat step 5 around points C, D, E, F, and G. Note that the points of the pattern at points W, X, Y, and Z will overlap each other.

Six Star Pattern 4

Using pearl cotton (coton perlé) #8 (coton á broder) for the pattern thread gives this design its delicate appearance.

MATERIALS
- 3-inch (70-80 mm) ball
- Red polyester sewing thread, 325 yards (300 m)
- Silver metallic thread, 5 yards (4 m)
- Pearl cotton (coton perlé) #8 (coton á broder), 23 yards (21 m) each of white, light blue, and medium blue

INSTRUCTIONS
1. Wrap and divide the ball into eight vertical sections with a line around the center to give you six centers.

2. Using metallic thread, apply the guidelines. Add two more guidelines at each pin, following the instructions on page 12, to give you four lines at each pin (creating eight spokes).

3. Beginning at point A, and following figure 1, plot points H, J, K, L, M, N, O, and P by placing a pin on each guideline approximately ¾ inch (2 cm) from point A.

4. Again following figure 1, enter the wrapped layer with the needle and thread so the thread exits below point H and just to the left of the guideline AD. Take the thread to point L and take a stitch, right to left. Then take a stitch at O, take a stitch at J, take a stitch at M, take a stitch at P, take a stitch at K, take a stitch at N, then back to H.

5. Continue to work the pattern in this way until the stitches reach almost to the guidelines that form the square around point A.

Figure 1

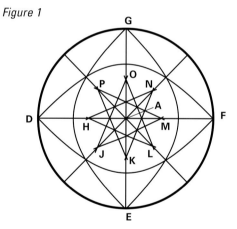

Figure 2

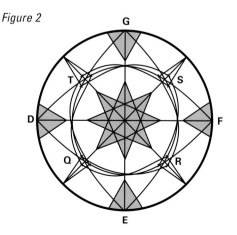

6. Repeat steps 3, 4, and 5 around points C, D, E, F, and G.

7. Following figure 2, plot points Q, R, S, and T by placing pins where the guidelines cross between each pattern. Use the strip of measuring paper to check that these pins are in the correct position.

8. Following steps 1 through 9 for Finishing the Ball on page 65, stitch the hexagonal pattern around the ball.

Six Star Pattern 5

Each star motif is a small square crossing pattern (see page 36) that is formed by alternately crossing bands of thread between points.

MATERIALS

- 3-inch (70-80 mm) ball
- Dark blue polyester sewing thread, 325 yards (300 m)
- Silver metallic thread, 9 yards (8 m)
- Fine silver metallic thread, 9 yards (8 m)
- Pearl cotton (coton perlé) #5, 1 skein = 27.3 yards (25 m), ³⁄₄ skein each of pink, medium turquoise, coral

INSTRUCTIONS

1. Wrap and divide the ball into eight vertical sections with a line around the center.

2. Using metallic thread, apply the guidelines. Add two more guidelines at each center pin, following the instructions on page 12, to give you four lines at each pin (creating eight spokes).

3. Following figure 1, plot points M, N, P, and Q by placing pins halfway between point A and the centerline on guidelines AD, AE, AF, and AG. These points will be the outer points of the pattern.

4. Plot points R, S, T, and U by placing pins halfway between point A and points M, N, P, and Q on guidelines AM, AN, AP, and AQ.

Figure 1

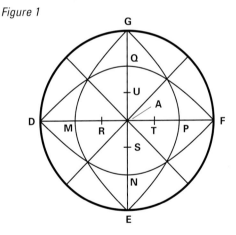

5. Thread two needles, each with a length of the same color thread. Enter the wrapped layer with the needle and thread so the needle exits below point R and just to the left of guideline AM. Lay the thread alongside the right of line RAT. Turn the ball so that point T is toward you. Take a stitch, right to left, at T. Lay the thread alongside the right of line TAR. Turn the ball so that point R is toward you and take a stitch at R. Continuing in this way, work two or three rounds in the first color. Make sure that the stitches are not too close to one another.

6. Next, go to the pin at point S and work as in step 5 with the other needle, working from point S to U and back to S.

7. Continue working with two needles, changing colors as desired, as you work alternately on pins R to T and S to U, until the stitching reaches points M and P, and N and Q, as shown in figure 2.

8. Repeat steps 3 through 7 around points C, D, E, F, and G. Note that when completed, the outer points of each pattern will touch the adjacent pattern.

9. To finish, use the fine silver thread to work the star motif between the stitched patterns.

Figure 2

Six Star Pattern 6

The star is a variation of the square crossing motif. The bands worked around it create an interesting octagon that frames the center of the star.

MATERIALS

- 3-inch (70-80 mm) ball
- Light lavender polyester sewing thread, 325 yards (300 m)
- Gold metallic thread, 9 yards (8 m)
- Fine gold metallic thread, 13 yards (12 m)
- Pearl cotton (coton perlé) #5, 1 skein = 27.3 yards (25 m), 1 skein each of dark red and green, ¾ skein of purple

INSTRUCTIONS

1. Wrap and divide the ball into eight vertical sections with a line around the center.

2. Using metallic thread, apply the guidelines. Add two more guidelines at each center pin, following the instructions on page 12, to give you four lines at each pin (creating eight spokes).

3. Following figure 1, plot points H, J, K, and L by placing pins on the diagonal guidelines halfway between point A and the corners of the squares that are formed by the guidelines.

4. Enter the wrapped layer with the needle and thread so the thread exits below the pin at point H just left of the guideline. Lay the thread alongside the right of line HAK. Turn the ball so that point K is toward you. Take a stitch, right to left, at K. Lay the thread alongside the right of line KAH. Turn the ball so that point H is toward you, and take a stitch at H.

5. Repeat step 4 between points J and L on line LAJ. Continue to work this way, alternating one round at HAK, followed by one round at LAJ. Work this pattern at all six points, A, C, D, E, F, and G, until the points of each pattern meet the adjacent patterns where the guideline threads cross.

Figure 1

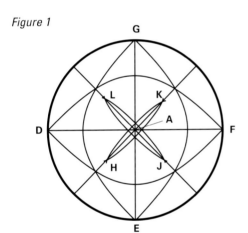

6. Return to point A. Following figure 2, plot points M, N, O, and P by moving the pins from points H, J, K, and L to the edges of the pattern as shown.

7. Plot points Q, R, S, and T by placing pins halfway between points M and D, N and E, O and F, and P and G.

8. Again following figure 2, enter the wrapped layer with the needle and thread so the needle exits below the pin at point Q and just to the left of the guideline. Take the thread to N and take a

stitch, right to left. Then take a stitch at S, take a stitch at P, and take a stitch at Q. Next, enter the wrapped layer with the needle and thread so the needle exits below the pin at point R and just to the left of the guideline. Take the thread to O and take a stitch, right to left. Then take a stitch at T, take a stitch at M, and take a stitch at R.

Figure 2

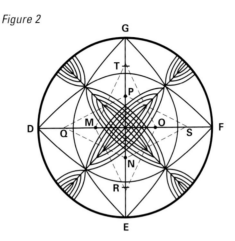

9. Continue stitching in this way, stitching one round on the first set of pins, Q, N, S, and P, then one round on the other set of pins, R, O, T, and M. Work this pattern until the points reach the square formed by the guidelines.

10. Repeat steps 6 through 9 around points C, D, E, F, and G. When completed, the points of all six patterns should meet.

11. To finish, use the fine metallic thread to work the star motif in the spaces between the points of the stars.

Six Star Pattern 7

Work the polystar pattern around each of the six centers to create this handsome design.

MATERIALS

- 3-inch (70-80 mm) ball
- Dark turquoise polyester sewing thread, 325 yards (300 m)
- Silver metallic thread, 18 yards (16 m)
- Fine silver metallic thread, 11 yards (10 m)
- Pearl cotton (coton perlé) #5, 1 skein = 27.3 yards (25 m), 1 skein each of red, white, light purple, and dark purple

INSTRUCTIONS

1. Wrap and divide the ball into eight vertical sections with a line around the center.

2. Using metallic thread, apply the guidelines. Add two more guidelines at each center pin, following the instructions on page 12, to give you four lines at each pin (creating eight spokes).

3. Following figure 1, plot points H, J, K, and L by placing pins on the diagonal guidelines halfway between point A and the corners of the squares that are formed by the guidelines. Plot points W, X, Y, and Z by placing pins as shown where the guidelines cross. Use the strip of measuring paper

to check that these last four points are all the same distance from point A.

4. Work the polystar pattern (see page 17) on these points. Begin by entering the wrapped layer with the needle and thread so the needle exits below the pin at point H and just to the left of the guideline. Take the thread to point A on AE and take a stitch, right to left, close to A. Then take a stitch at J, take a stitch close to A on AF, take a stitch at K, take a stitch close to A on AG, take a stitch at L, take a stitch close to A on AD, then back to H. Continue working this way until the stitching reaches points W, X, Y, and Z.

5. Repeat step 4 around points C, D, E, F, and G. When completed, the points of each pattern should meet the points of the adjacent patterns.

Figure 1

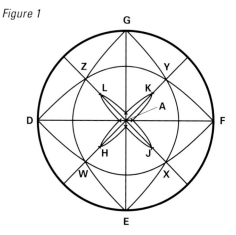

Figure 2

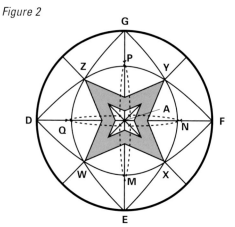

6. Following figure 2, return to point A and plot points M, N, P, and Q by placing pins on the guidelines that are between points W, X, Y, and Z.

7. As you did in step 4, work the polystar pattern on these points. Begin at point M, then take a stitch close to A on AX, take a stitch at N, take a stitch close to A on AY, take a stitch at P, take a stitch close to A on AZ, take a stitch at Q, take a stitch close to A on AW, then back to M.

Continuing to work this way, work four or five rounds around point A.

8. Repeat steps 6 and 7 around points C, D, E, F, and G. Note that the points of the motif will overlap the points of the adjacent motifs.

9. To finish, use the fine metallic thread to work the star motif between the points of the motifs.

Banded Pattern 1

Whether you work this pattern on a large ball using pearl cotton (coton perlé) #5, or on a small ball using a thinner thread, the wide bands of color create a bold design.

MATERIALS

Red and Blue Ball
- 2- or 2½-inch (50-65 mm) ball
- Red polyester sewing thread, 217 yards (200 m)
- Gold metallic thread, 4½ yards (4 m)
- Fine gold metallic thread, 4½ yards (4 m)
- Pearl cotton (coton perlé) #8 (coton á broder), 9 yards (8 m) each of white and dark blue, 7½ yards (7 m) of light green

Blue and Rose Ball
- 3-inch (70-80 mm) ball
- Light blue polyester sewing thread, 325 yards (300 m)
- Gold metallic thread, 10 yards (9 m)
- Fine gold thread, 9 yards (8 m)
- Pearl cotton (coton perlé) #5, 1 skein=27.3 yards (25 m), ½ skein each of medium pink, navy blue, and dark rose, ¼ skein of medium green

INSTRUCTIONS

1. Wrap the ball and divide it into eight vertical sections.

2. Using metallic thread, apply the guidelines. Add two more guidelines at each of the four center pins around the central guideline, following the instructions on page 12, to give you four lines at each pin (creating eight spokes).

3. Enter the wrapped layer with the needle and thread so the needle exits at the pin at point A.

4. Wind the thread around the ball, taking care that it lies flat against the center guideline. Wind on as many rounds as desired of the first color, making sure that the threads lie close to one another. Finish winding at point A.

Figure 1

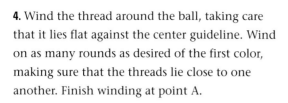

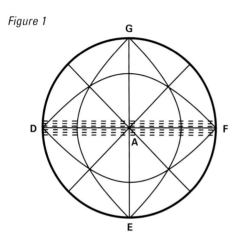

5. Pass the needle beneath the first rounds so that it exits on the other side of the guideline. As in step 4, wind the thread around the ball as shown in figure 1. Fasten the thread off by taking two long stitches through the wrapping threads.

Figure 2

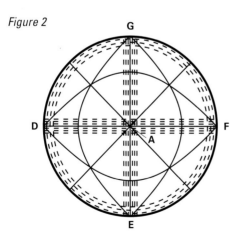

6. Following figure 2, repeat steps 3 through 5 around the guideline with points E, C, G, and A, then the guideline with points D, E, F, and G.

7. Thread the needle with another color. As in steps 3 to 6, wind an equal number of rounds on both sides of the bands. Repeat, using a third color. You know the bands are wide enough when the threads of the last round begin to slip off the ball; at this point, stop winding.

8. To prevent the bands from slipping off, work the herringbone stitch in a square at the intersection of the threads as shown in figure 3.

9. To finish, use the fine metallic thread to work a star motif within the triangular spaces between the bands of thread.

Figure 3

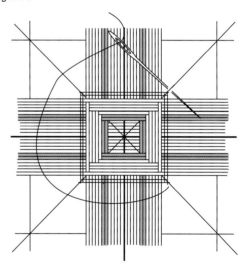

Figure 1

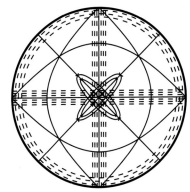

Banded Pattern 2

This design is a variation of Banded Pattern 1 on page 97. The ball is wrapped with a thicker crochet cotton to give the wrapped layer more texture.

MATERIALS
- 3-inch (70-75 mm) ball
- White crochet cotton, 325 yards (300 m)
- Pearl cotton (coton perlé) #5, 1 skein = 27.3 yards (25 m), ½ skein each of dark green and red, ¾ skein of yellow, ¼ skein of medium green

INSTRUCTIONS

1. Follow steps 1 through 7 for Banded Pattern 1 on pages 97 and 98. Use pearl cotton (coton perlé) for applying the guidelines rather than metallic thread.

2. Following figure 1, stitch across the intersection of the threads. Alternate rounds, working one round in one direction, and one round in the other. You want the threads to cross as in a square crossing pattern (see page 36).

3. Using pearl cotton (coton perlé), work a star motif within each triangular space between the bands of thread.

Banded Triangles

This design combines a banded pattern with interlocking triangles to create an intricate-looking design that's easy to make.

MATERIALS

White, Red, and Green Ball

- 2- or 2½ inch (50-65 mm) ball
- White polyester sewing thread, 217 yards (200 m)
- Gold metallic thread, 4½ yards (4 m)
- Fine gold metallic thread, 9 yards (8 m)
- Pearl cotton (coton perlé) #5, 1 skein = 27.3 yards (25 m), ½ skein each of red, light blue, dark blue, and medium green

Red, Green, and Beige Ball

- 3-inch (70-80 mm) ball
- Red polyester sewing thread, 325 yards (300 m)
- Gold metallic thread, 11 yards (10 m)
- Pearl cotton (coton perlé) #5, 1 skein = 27.3 yards (25 m), ½ skein each of beige, medium pink, dark coral, and olive green

INSTRUCTIONS

1. Follow steps 1 through 8 for Banded Pattern 1 on pages 97 and 98.

2. Following figure 1, plot points X, Y, and Z by placing pins outside of the bands of thread. These points will be the points of the first triangle.

3. Using contrasting colors of thread, stitch the first triangle on points X, Y, and Z, by stitching outside the pins. Change colors as desired, but do not work too many rounds or the bands of the triangles will overwhelm the pattern worked in step 1. Complete one triangle before progressing to the next.

4. Reposition the pins X, Y, and Z to form a second triangle, and work as in steps 2 and 3 until you have eight triangles around the ball. To make the triangles intertwine, you will need to alternately pass the needle and thread over and under the threads of the previously worked triangle.

5. When all the triangles have been worked, you can finish the ball by using fine metallic thread to work a star motif in the space at the center of each triangle.

Figure 1

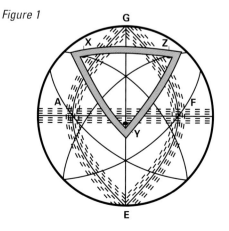

Banded Pattern 3

This pattern is similar to Banded Pattern 1 on page 97. While there is little stitching, you will need to weave each round alternately over and under the previous round. This makes the ball slower to work, but the interesting results make it worth the effort.

MATERIALS

- 3-inch (70-80 mm) ball
- Beige polyester sewing thread, 325 yards (300 m)
- Gold metallic thread, 3½ yards (3 m)
- Fine gold metallic thread, 9 yards (8 m)
- Pearl cotton (coton perlé) #5, 1 skein = 27.3 yards (25 m), ¾ skein each in mauve, dark blue, and light blue

INSTRUCTIONS

1. Wrap the ball and divide it into eight vertical sections with a line around the center. Keep a pin at each of the six centers.

2. Using metallic thread, apply the guidelines. Add two more guidelines at each pin, following the instructions on page 12, to give you four lines at each pin (creating eight spokes).

3. Since the thread is wound around the ball, you do not want to fasten off too many times. To avoid this, work with as long a length of thread as is manageable. Following figure 1, begin by

winding two rounds of the first color beside line AECG. Leave a space of approximately ¼ inch (.75 cm) between the guideline and the working thread. Wind two rounds of the same color on the other side of the same guideline.

Figure 1

4. Repeat step 3 on both sides of the guidelines DEFG and ADCF. *Whenever a thread crosses another, it must go alternately over or under it. If these lines should slip, place pins into the ball to temporarily hold them in place.*

Figure 2

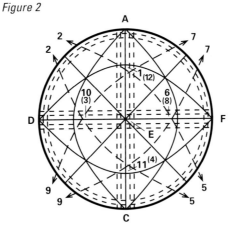

5. Following figure 2, wind two rounds of the first color diagonally around 1, 2, 3, 4, 5, 6; then 1, 7, 8, 4, 9, 10; then 11, 10, 2, 12, 8, 5; then 11, 6, 7,

12, 3, 9, 11. You may find it helpful to mark the ball first with small pieces of paper that are numbered to correspond to the points. Remember to always weave over and under each band of threads. You must get this correct in the first rounds since it will affect the subsequent rounds. While the weaving over and under should stop the threads from slipping off the ball, take up a little of the wrapping thread with the needle when going under a band of threads as an extra precaution.

6. Return to the first band worked in step 3, and wind on a second color on the outside (the side away from the guideline) of the first two rounds. Repeat steps 4 and 5 using the second color, then repeat steps 3 and 4 using a third color. Note: for the ball in the photograph, I omitted the three rounds of the third color from the four diagonal bands.

7. If desired, use a fine metallic thread to work a star motif on the stars that are already formed where the guidelines cross.

Triangles

The visual unity of this design is in the small squares that form around each center. They create interesting meeting points for the bands of color that encircle the ball. Work this pattern on a smaller 2-inch (50 mm) ball using pearl cotton #8 (coton á broder).

MATERIALS

- 2- or 2½-inch (50-65 mm) ball
- Emerald green polyester sewing thread, 217 yards (200 m)
- Silver metallic thread, 3½ yards (3 m)
- Fine silver metallic thread, 6 yards (5 m)
- Fine red metallic thread, 6 yards (5 m)
- Pearl cotton (coton perlé) #8 (coton á broder), 15 yards (14 m) each of white, navy blue, and medium rose

INSTRUCTIONS

1. Wrap the ball and divide it into eight vertical sections with a line around the center.

2. Using metallic thread, apply the guidelines. Add two more guidelines at each pin, following the instructions on page 12, to give you four lines at each pin (creating eight spokes).

3. Following figure 1, stitch a triangle around the pins at points A, E, and F. Make the stitches on the outside of the pins, taking care to stitch under the center guideline at each point. Continue working rounds in this color until the band is a few threads wide. Working in the same way as above, work a triangle around pins A, G, and D.

4. As you did in step 3, work triangles around points C, F, and G, and C, D, and E. Note that these points are not shown in figure 1 since they are on the other side of the ball.

5. Change the thread color. Return to the first triangle and work rounds to create a band that is a few threads wide. Work this second color in the same way around the other triangles. Change to a third color and repeat. You may vary the number of threads for each band of color as desired.

6. Finish the ball by working the star motif in the spaces between the triangles. For this ball, I used both metallic silver and red thread to work the star motifs.

Figure 1

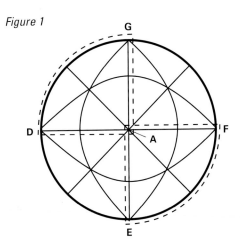

Triangles 2

The small triangles worked in metallic thread accentuate the small hexagons that are formed by the stitched bands.

MATERIALS

- 3-inch (70-80 mm) ball
- Dark green polyester sewing thread, 325 yards (300 m)
- Gold metallic thread, 8 yards (7 m)
- Fine gold metallic thread, 9 yards (8 m)
- Pearl cotton (coton perlé) #5, 1 skein = 27.3 yards (25 m), ⅓ skein each of red, light blue, and pink

INSTRUCTIONS

1. Wrap the ball and divide it into eight vertical sections with a line around the center. Use the red pins for marking the top and bottom points; use white pins for marking the points around the center.

2. Using metallic thread, apply the guidelines. Add two more guidelines at each of the four pins around the centerline to give you four lines at each pin (creating eight spokes).

3. Using green pins, and the strip of measuring paper, follow figure 1 to plot points H, J, K, and L, and M, N, O, and P at the points where the guidelines cross. Using the paper strip guarantees

that the pins are all at the same distance from points A and C. Since you will be stitching around these eight points, you may find it helpful to pin small pieces of paper labeled with the appropriate letter to all points.

4. Again following figure 1, enter the wrapped layer with the needle and thread so the needle exits below point H and just to the left of guideline HD. Take the next stitch at N on guideline NC. Take the next stitch at K on guideline KG. Note the point K is on the other side of the ball. Then return to H. This will complete one round. Note: The thread is laid alongside the guidelines to form a triangle, and the stitches are taken centrally between the lines at the points of the triangle. This will be the same for all triangles.

Figure 1

```
            A
    from K   H      J
          (L)   (K)
    D          E          F
          (P)   (O)
        M          N     to K
            C
```

5. Stitch similar large triangles around points H, K, and P; then J, L, and M; then J, O, and L. Note that these triangles each pass the top point A.

6. Repeat steps 4 and 5 around point C, stitching on points M, O, and J; M, O, and L; P, K, and N; and P, N, and H. Return to point H in step 4 and repeat steps 4, 5, and 6.

7. Repeat steps 4 through 6 using a second color, then a third. The photograph shows a ball worked with six rounds (two rounds each of three colors) for each triangle. Note: It will be seen that the stitches are taken on the guidelines between the colored thread.

8. Following figure 2, plot points 1, 2, 3, and 4 around point A by placing pins on the four guidelines approximately ¾ inch (2 cm) from point A. Then stitch from point 1 to 3, then from 3 to 1. Do this twice. Next, stitch from point 2 to 4 and from 4 to 2. Do this twice. This stitching should prevent the previous bands from slipping off the ball.

Figure 2

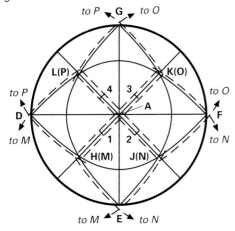

9. Repeat step 8 at all six points where the bands of thread cross one another.

10. To make the triangles around the hexagons, plot points 5, 6, and 7 by placing pins approximately ¾ inch (2 cm) from the hexagon. Then plot points 8, 9, and 10 by placing pins at the edge of the hexagon on the same guidelines. See figure 3.

11. Using the metallic thread you used for the guidelines, stitch from point 5 to 9, from 9 to 7, from 7 to 8, from 8 to 6, from 6 to 10, and from 10 to 5. Work two rounds. Then repeat this step at all eight points around the ball.

12. To finish, use the fine metallic thread to work a star motif in each of the 12 spaces between the patterns.

Figure 3

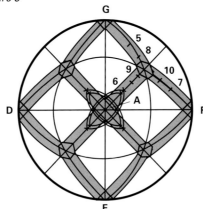

Overlapping Triangles

Work this pattern on a smaller 2- or 2½-inch (50-65 mm) ball using pearl cotton (coton perlé) #8 (coton á broder).

MATERIALS

- 2- or 2½-inch (50-65 mm) ball
- Yellow-green polyester sewing thread, 216 yards (200 m)
- Gold metallic thread, 5½ yards (5 m)
- Pearl cotton (coton perlé) #8 (coton á broder), 15 yards (14 m) each of red, white, and purple

INSTRUCTIONS

1. Wrap the ball and divide it into eight vertical sections with a line around the center.

2. Using metallic thread, apply the guidelines. Add two more guidelines at each pin, following the instructions on page 12, to give you four lines at each pin (creating eight spokes).

3. Following figure 1, work first around the pins at points A, E, and F to stitch a triangle outside of the pins. Take care to stitch under the center guidelines only. When you have worked two or three rounds, stitch a similar triangle around points A, D, and G, then around points C, F, and G, then around points C, D, and E.

4. Return to the first triangle around points A, E, and F, and work some rounds in other colors. Then repeat these same colors around the other triangles in order, working around A, D, and G, then C, F, and G, then C, D, and E.

5. Following figure 2, plot points H, J, K; L, M, N; O, P, Q; and R, S, T. Note that points O, P, Q and R, S, T are not shown in the diagram since they are on the other side of the ball. Place the pins outside of the threads of the triangles, positioning them halfway between the corners of the triangles. Use the strip of measuring paper to make sure they are accurately placed.

Figure 1

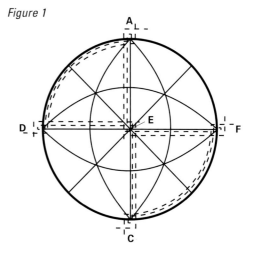

Figure 2

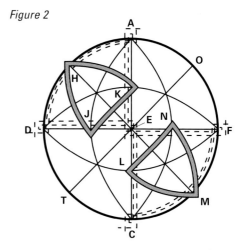

6. As you did in step 3, stitch triangles around the outside of these pins.

7. Following figure 3, return to the first triangle AEF, and reposition the pins K, O, and N to be on the other side of the lines AE, EF, and FA. As before, stitch a triangle of three or four rounds around points K, O, and N.

8. Go to triangle DEC and reposition the pins J, L, and T so they are on the other side of the lines ED, DC, and CE. Stitch a triangle with the same number of rounds as in step 7 around these pins. Repeat this at triangle CFG, repositioning the pins M, P, and R so they are on the other side of the lines FC, CG, and GF. Repeat this at triangle AGD, repositioning the pins H, S, and Q so they are on the other side of the lines AG, GD, and DA.

Figure 3

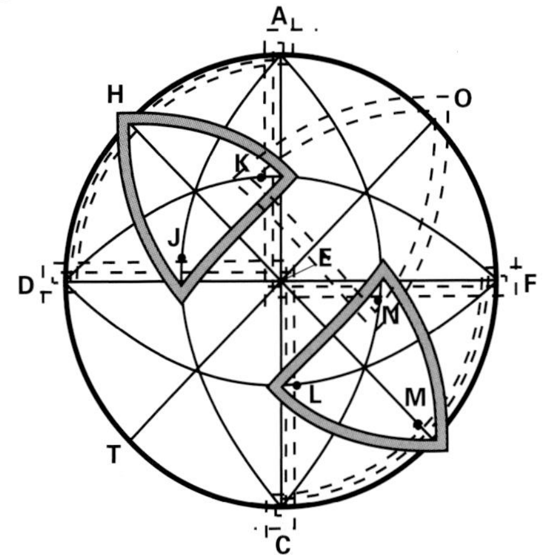

9. To finish, stitch a star motif in the center of each of the four triangles.

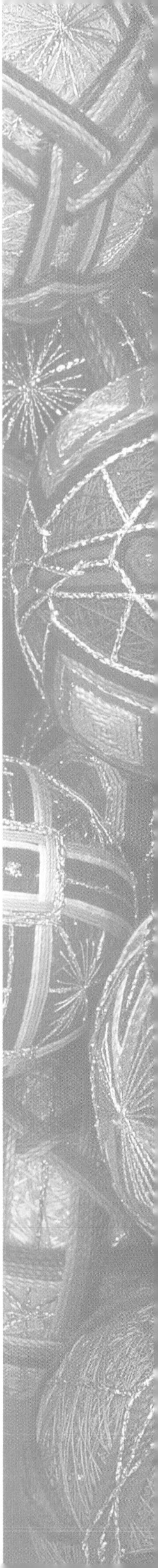

Patterns Around
Eight & Twelve Centers

Eight Centers

This pattern is worked around eight centers. Once you plot the centers, you'll wrap and stitch the threads around the ball from point to point to create the design. Using a larger 4-inch ball (100 mm), as shown here, allows for a nice balance between the wrapping layer and the pattern.

MATERIALS

- 4-inch (100 mm) ball
- Light blue polyester sewing thread, 433 yards (400 m)
- Gold metallic thread, 4½ yards (4 m)
- Fine gold metallic thread, 13 yards (12 m)
- Pearl cotton (coton perlé) #5, 1 skein = 27.3 yards (25 m), 1 skein each of purple and emerald green, ½ skein of navy blue

INSTRUCTIONS

1. Wrap the ball and divide it into six vertical sections. Apply the guidelines using metallic thread.

2. Following figure 1, plot points D, E, F, G, H, and J by placing pins on the vertical guidelines, alternating between one-third and two-thirds the length of the guideline from point A. Points D, F,

and H will be one-third of the length from point A, while points E, G, and J will be two-thirds of the length. Note that points G, H, and J are on the other side of the ball. Points A, C, D, E, F, G, H, and J create the eight centers. You now need three guidelines (creating six spokes) passing through each center; apply the additional guidelines. To help you work around the ball, write the letters A, C, D, E, F, G, H, and J on small squares of paper and pin them to the corresponding points.

Figure 1

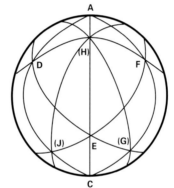

Figure 2

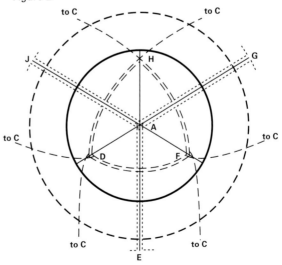

3. Following figure 2, stitch the first color from point A to E to G to A, taking the stitches on guidelines AJ, EJ, and GJ. This will form a large triangle. The figure shows three rounds of the first color.

4. Next, stitch the rounds of the first color from A to G to J to A, taking the stitches on guidelines AE, GE, and JE.

5. Then stitch the rounds of the first color from A to J to E to A, taking the stitches on guidelines AG, JG, and EG.

6. Stitch the rounds of the first color from H to D to F to H, taking the stitches on guidelines HC, DC, and FC.

7. Stitch the rounds of the first color from C to F to D to C, taking the stitches on guidelines CH, FH, and DH.

8. Stitch the rounds of the first color from C to D to H to C, taking the stitches on guidelines CF, DF, and HF.

9. Stitch the rounds of the first color from C to H to F to C, taking the stitches on guidelines CD, HD, and FD.

10. Stitch the rounds of the first color from G to E to J to G, taking stitches on guidelines GA, EA, and JA.

11. Repeat steps 3 through 10 in the second and third choice of colors. Note: Once you've completed the sequence in Steps 3 to 10, the stitching at the centers will form a hexagon with the triangles overlapping each other halfway between these points, and the overlapping threads will form a square between each hexa-

gon. Following figure 3, stitch a square around the square formed by the overlapping threads.

12. Following figure 4, stitch across the hexagons formed at the eight centers. Note that there are three lines of stitching.

13. To finish, use fine metallic thread to work the star motif in the spaces between the pattern thread.

Figure 3

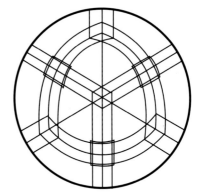

Figure 4

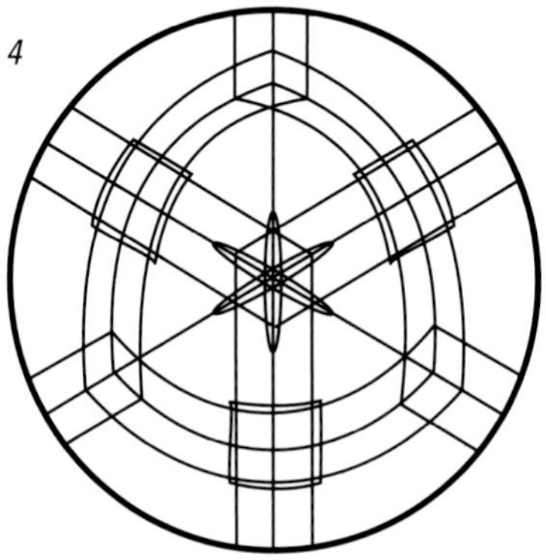

Twelve Centers Pentagon Pattern 1

The 12 centers for this pattern are plotted on alternate guidelines, with five points marked toward the top of the ball and five points toward the bottom; points A and C are also two of the centers. Except for the project on page 117, the points for 12 centers in all the following projects are plotted the same way.

MATERIALS

- 3-inch (70-80 mm) ball
- White polyester sewing thread, 325 yards (300 m)
- Gold metallic thread, 9 yards (8 m)
- Fine gold metallic thread, 13 yards (12 m)
- Pearl cotton (coton perlé) #5, 1 skein = 27.3 yards (25 m), ½ skein each of dark blue, pink, and dark rose

INSTRUCTIONS

1. Wrap the ball and divide it into 10 vertical sections. Using metallic thread, apply the guidelines. You do not need a line around the center, but keep the pins around the center for now.

2. Using the strip of measuring paper, divide the length of guideline AC into three equal parts. Pin the paper back onto the ball at point A. Following figure 1, plot points D, E, F, G, H, J, K, L, M, and N. For points D, F, H, K, and M, place pins on alternate guidelines that are one-third of the length of the guideline from point A. Note that points K and M are on the other side of the ball. For points E, G, J, L, and N place pins on the remaining guidelines that are two-thirds of the length of the guidelines from point A. Note that points J and L are on the other side of the ball.

3. Remove any pins from around the center of the ball. The remaining pins mark the 12 centers of the pentagons.

Figure 1

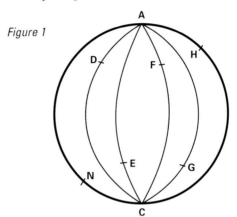

4. In order to work the pentagons, each of the points will need 10 spokes. To do this, use a long length of thread and begin at point D. Wind the thread around the ball until five lines cross at D (creating 10 spokes). Take two or three small stitches where the threads cross to secure.

5. Move to point F, and as you did in step 4, add rounds of thread to create 10 spokes at this point. Continue in this way until all points have 10 spokes.

6. Following figure 2, plot points O, P, Q, R, and S. Begin by pinning the strip of measuring paper at point A. Divide the length of guideline AD in half by bringing the mark for one-third of the length of the guideline (see step 2) up to point A and making a fold in the paper. Using the fold as the measuring point from point A, place a pin at the fold on each of the guidelines AD, AF, AH, AK, and AM. These points, O, P, Q, R, and S, are the points around which you will work the pentagon. Plot the points for each pentagon in the same way around the 12 centers.

Figure 2

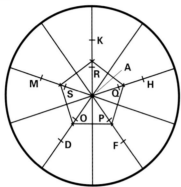

7. Begin working around point A. Stitch counterclockwise around the outside of the five points O, P, Q, R, and S, taking each stitch from right to left.

8. Progress from one center to the next, working the desired number of rounds in the chosen colors. The pentagons will overlap one another. As shown in figure 3, one pentagon is stitched first, then subsequent pentagons may be woven over and under as they are stitched. Or, each pentagon can lie on top of the next pentagon.

Figure 3

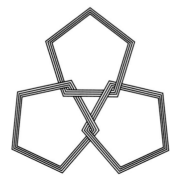

9. To finish, use the fine metallic thread to work the star motif in the center of each pentagon.

> **TIP:** *It is easier to work the first rounds in the first color on all 12 pentagons before changing to the next color. As soon as two overlapping pentagons have been stitched, remove the pin between them. This will reduce the number of pins in the ball during stitching.*

Twelve Centers Pentagon Pattern 2

Like Pentagon Pattern 1 on page 111 each pentagon is worked around one of the 12 centers. The much different look for this project is easily achieved by working the motif out from a central point, rather than working it around the outer points of the pentagon.

MATERIALS

- 3-inch (70-80 mm) ball
- Medium blue-green polyester sewing thread, 325 yards (300 m)
- Silver metallic thread, 9 yards (8 m)
- Fine silver metallic thread, 13 yards (12 m)
- Pearl cotton (coton perlé) #5, 1 skein = 27.3 yards (25 m), ½ skein each of light rose, pink, navy, white, and deep rose

INSTRUCTIONS

1. Work steps 1 through 6 for Pentagon Pattern 1 on page 111.

2. Beginning at center point A, work a pentagon out from the central pin toward the pins at points O, P, Q, R, and S. See figure 2 on page 112.

3. Repeat step 2 around all remaining center points.

4. To finish, use the fine metallic thread to work a star motif in each of the triangular spaces between the pentagons.

Twelve Centers Star

Repeating the same motif around 12 centers makes this pattern look more intricate than it is to work. As shown, the project is worked in pearl cotton (coton perlé) #5. Since each motif is quite small, you could work the pattern in pearl cotton (coton perlé) #8 (coton á broder) for a different look.

MATERIALS

- 3-inch ball (70-80 mm)
- Light blue polyester sewing thread, 325 yards (300 m)
- Silver metallic thread, 22 yards (20 m)
- Fine silver metallic thread, 13 yards (12 m)
- Pearl cotton (coton perlé) #5, 1 skein = 27.3 yards (25 m), ½ skein each of blue, medium lavender, and dark rose.

INSTRUCTIONS

1. Wrap and divide the ball into 10 vertical sections. Use the same color pin for the top and bottom points. Using metallic thread, apply the guidelines.

2. Following figure 1, plot points D, E, F, G, H, J, K, L, M, and N. For points D, F, H, K, and M, place pins on alternate guidelines at one-third of the length of the guideline from point A. Note that points K and M are on the other side of the ball. For points E, G, J, L, and N, place pins on the remaining guidelines at two-thirds of the length of the guidelines from point A. Note that points J and L are on the other side of the ball. Points A, C, D, E, F, G, H, J, K, L, M, and N are the 12 centers of the pattern.

Figure 1

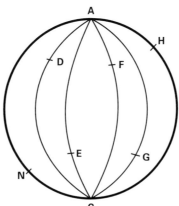

3. Apply additional guidelines so there are five guidelines (creating 10 spokes) passing through each center.

4. Following figure 2, begin around point A and stitch a solid pentagon of approximately five rounds, or until it extends ¼ inch (.5 cm) from point A. With 10 vertical sections, you can easily stitch a pentagon by stitching on alternate guidelines.

Figure 2

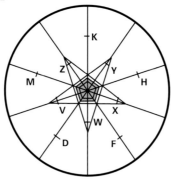

5. Again following figure 2, plot points V, W, X, Y, and Z by placing pins on alternate guidelines ½ inch (1.5 cm) from point A.

Figure 3

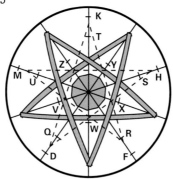

6. Stitch the star by entering the wrapped layer with the needle and thread so the needle exits to the left of the guideline and just below the pin at point V, then take a stitch, right to left, at X. Stitch from X to Z, from Z to W, from W to Y,

and from Y to V. Continuing to work this way, stitch four rounds.

7. Following figure 3, plot points Q, R, S, T, and U by repositioning the pins, placing them approximately ⅝ inch (1.75 cm) from point A.

8. Again following figure 3, and as you did in step 6, stitch from Q to S, from S to U, from U to R, from R to T, and from T to Q. Continuing to work this way, stitch three or four rounds.

9. Stitch this pattern around the remaining 11 centers.

10. To finish, use the fine metallic thread to work a small star motif in each of the spaces between the points of the stars.

Twelve Centers Wrapped Bands 1

As you work this pattern, a pentagon forms around points A and C, while a diamond forms around each of the other points. Since the threads do not lie close to one another, it's best to work this pattern on a smaller ball.

MATERIALS

- 3-inch (70-80 mm) ball
- Light blue polyester sewing thread, 325 yards (300 m)
- Silver metallic thread, 9 yards (8 m)
- Pearl cotton (coton perlé) #5, 1 skein = 27.3 yards (25 m), ¼ skein each of white, blue, and red

INSTRUCTIONS

1. Wrap the ball and divide it into 10 vertical sections. Using the metallic thread, apply the guidelines.

Figure 1

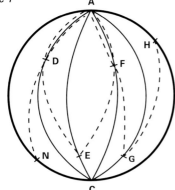

2. Following figure 1, plot points D, E, F, G, H, J, K, L, M, and N. For points D, F, H, K, and M, place pins on alternate guidelines that are one-third of the length of the guideline from point A. Note that points K and M are on the other side of the ball. For points E, G, J, L, and N, place pins on the remaining guidelines that are two-thirds of the length of the guidelines from point A. Note that points J and L are on the other side of the ball.

3. Apply five additional guidelines to each point (creating 10 spokes).

4. Again following figure 1, begin to stitch the pattern by entering the wrapped layer with the needle and thread so the needle exits to the left

of line AD close to point A. Stitch from A to D to E to F to A in the first color.

5. Next, also in the first color, stitch from A to F to G to H to A. Repeat steps 4 and 5 until you have stitched five diamonds around point A.

6. As you did in steps 4 and 5, work five diamonds around point C. Change to your second color and repeat steps 4 to 6.

7. Change to your third color and repeat steps 4 through 6.

Twelve Centers Wrapped Bands 2

With this pattern, you'll find it helpful to number each pentagon so you can easily keep track of your position on the ball as you work.

MATERIALS

- 3-inch (70-80 mm) ball
- Dark blue polyester sewing thread, 300 yards (325 m)
- Silver metallic thread, 9 yards (8 m)
- Fine silver metallic thread, 13 yards (12 m)
- Pearl cotton (coton perlé) #5, 1 skein = 27.3 yards (25 m), ½ skein each of light blue, medium blue, and magenta

INSTRUCTIONS

1. Wrap the ball and divide it into 10 vertical divisions. Using the metallic thread, apply the guidelines.

2. Following figure 1, plot points D, E, F, G, H, J, K, L, M, and N. For points D, F, H, K, and M, place pins on alternate guidelines at one-third of the length of the guideline from point A. Note that points K and M are on the other side of the ball. For points E, G, J, L, and N, place pins on the remaining guidelines at two-thirds of the length of the guidelines from point A. Note that points J and K are on the other side of the ball. Check that the distances A to D, D to E, E to C, and E to F are all equal. It may be necessary to slightly adjust the position of the pins.

3. Apply five metallic threads to each point (creating 10 spokes). These points will be the center of each pentagon.

4. Following figure 2, plot points 1, 2, 3, 4, and 5 approximately ¾ inch (2 cm) from point A. Use pins in another color from those already used. Do the same around each of the other 11 points where six spokes cross. These pins mark the outer points of each pentagon, and should be of equal distance from the center pins.

5. Again following figure 2, and with your first color of thread, stitch from pin to pin, stitching outside the pins, around point A. Stitch a band of approximately six rounds altogether in a variety of colors.

6. Repeat step 5 around each of the points, C, D, E, F, G, H, J, K, L, M, and N. You'll find it easier to work the pentagon around A, then proceed to the five adjacent pentagons; then work the pentagon around C, followed by those five adjacent pentagons.

As you stitch every subsequent round, remember to take the thread alternately under, then over previous bands of thread. Note that it is easy to make a mistake at this stage. If you do make a mistake, don't worry too much about it. This pattern is forgiving; the mistakes aren't obvious if the weaving is occasionally incorrect.

7. To finish, note that the shapes within the pentagons already have a star formed by the spokes of thread. If desired, use a finer metallic thread to add additional spokes to make a more glittery star.

Figure 1

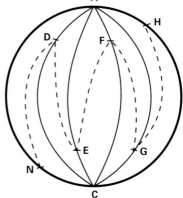

Figure 2

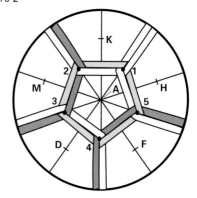

Twelve Center Cube

Consider this pattern a circle in a square. As you work the hexagons around the 12 centers, squares form, giving you the illusion of cubes circling the ball. Note that the 12 centers are plotted differently than the other patterns with 12 centers.

MATERIALS

- 3-inch (70-80 mm) ball
- Medium turquoise polyester sewing thread, 325 yards (300 m)
- Silver metallic thread, 4½ yards (4 m)
- Fine silver metallic thread, 11 yards (10 m)
- Pearl cotton (coton perlé) #5, 1 skein = 27.3 yards (25 m), ¾ skein each of dark purple and pale gray-green

INSTRUCTIONS

1. Wrap the ball and divide it into eight vertical sections with a line around the center.

2. Using metallic thread, apply the guidelines. Add two more guidelines at each of the four points, D, F, H, and K, around the center (creating eight spokes).

3. Following figure 1, plot points M, N, O, and P, by placing the pins so that guidelines AP = PD = DM = MA etc. The guidelines from points A to P to D to M are the outer edges of the first diamond shape.

4. In this pattern you want to stitch from inside the pins outward. Therefore, it is necessary to plot points 1, 2, 3, and 4 by placing the pins approximately ⅜ inch (1 cm) in from points A, P, D, and M, as shown in figure 1.

5. Stitch two rounds in the first color around pins 1, 2, 3, and 4. This will make a diamond shape. Stitch similar diamonds inside the diamond shapes between points AMFN, ANHO, and AOKP, as shown in figure 2.

6. Repeat steps 3 through 5 around point C.

Figure 1

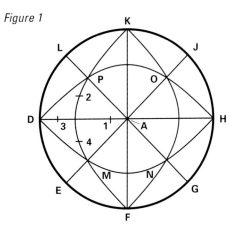

7. Following figure 3, stitch four diamond shapes around the centerline around the lines between points DMFQ, FNHR, HOKS, and KPDT. Points HOKS and KPDT are on the other side of the ball.

Figure 2

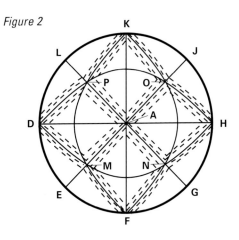

8. Following figure 3, stitch hexagons around points M, N, O, and P, and points Q, R, S, and T. Points O and P and S and T are on the other side of the ball. Note that this pattern requires many pins. After you complete this step, you can remove all the pins. If the basic wrapping thread is both firm and quite dense, the stitches will not slip.

9. Return to the first diamond shape and repeat steps 4 through 8 using the second color and completing two rounds.

10. Repeat steps 4 through 9 until you have four bands (two rounds of each color) of thread around each shape.

11. To finish, use the fine metallic thread to work the star motif in the spaces between each diamond motif.

Figure 3

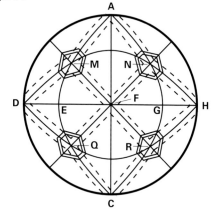

Twelve Centers Triangle Pattern

With so many centers, each motif is quite small. Working the pattern on a larger ball shows the design to its best advantage.

MATERIALS

- 4-inch (100 mm) ball
- Light blue polyester sewing thread, 433 yards (400 m)
- Gold metallic thread, 13 yards (12 m)
- Pearl cotton (coton perlé) #5, 1 skein = 27.3 yards (25 m), ¾ skein each in pale coral, light blue, and black, ½ skein in medium coral.

INSTRUCTIONS

1. Wrap the ball and divide it into 10 vertical sections. Use the same color pins for the top and bottom points. Using metallic thread, apply the guidelines. Remove the pins around the centerline.

2. Following figure 1, plot points D, E, F, G, H, J, K, L, M, and N. For points D, F, H, K, and M, place pins on alternate guidelines that are one-third of the length of the guideline from point A. Note that points K and M are on the other side of the ball. For points E, G, J, L, and N, place pins on the remaining guidelines that are two-thirds of the length of the guidelines from point A. Note that points J and L are on the other side of the ball.

3. Apply five additional guidelines to each point (creating 10 spokes).

4. Working around point A first, there are five triangles created by the pins D, F, H, K, M, with A. Place a pin in the center of each triangle; this will be where the guidelines cross. To measure this accurately, use the strip of measuring paper and pin the top point of the strip to point A. The center of the top five triangles, as shown in figure 2, will be at the first 1/10th mark on the paper strip.

5. Working at the top of the ball only, use the first color to stitch a triangle around each pin. Work the desired number of rounds in the first color to create the central triangle for each of these five triangles.

6. Repeat steps 4 and 5 around point C.

7. Plot the centers of the remaining triangles around the center of the ball. As you did in steps 4 and 5, work the desired number of rounds in the first color to create the central triangle for each of these triangles.

8. When the center color of all the triangles has been stitched, return to the first set of triangles around point A and complete the stitching in the second color. Then work around point C, then around the center to finish all the triangles. There will be 20 triangles altogether. Leave a narrow strip between the triangles so the wrapping thread will show through.

9. To create the star between the triangles, return to the pins that are at the centers of the 10 spokes, and work two or three rounds of the polystar pattern at each point.

Figure 1

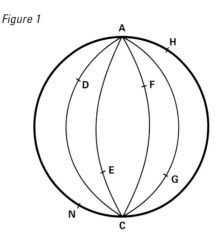

Figure 2

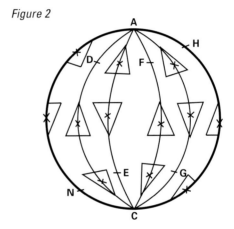

Eggs & Other Patterns

Egg Pattern 1

The egg shape provides another way to use your techniques. You'll find, however, that there are limitations to the patterns you can use because the shape is not symmetrical. Variations on the polystar patterns around two centers seem to work best. This pattern was worked on a larger egg shape that is 6 inches (15 cm) in length.

MATERIALS

- 6-inch (15 cm) polystyrene egg
- Beige polyester sewing thread, 650 yards (600 m)
- Gold metallic thread, 12 yards (11 m)
- Pearl cotton (coton perlé) #5, 1 skein = 27.3 yards (25 m), 1 skein each of white and yellow, ³⁄₄ skein each of light orange and dark orange

INSTRUCTIONS

1. Wrap the egg. Using a strip of measuring paper, plot the top and bottom points. You will need to plot the top point by placing the pin by eye. Take time to ensure that the top and bottom pins are in the correct position. Use the strip of measuring paper to check the distance between the top and bottom pins at short intervals all the way around the egg. Adjust the pins as necessary.

2. Plot a line around the center. Measure this distance and mark it on a second strip of paper.

3. Divide the egg into 12 sections. To do this, use the second strip of paper and divide it into 12 sections to plot 12 equally spaced points around the center of the egg. Using the metallic thread, apply the guidelines.

4. Following figure 1, stitch a polystar pattern around the top and bottom points. Stitch alternate rounds, first on one set of guidelines, then on the guidelines in between. Continue working in this way until the pattern is approximately 1 inch (2.5 cm) from the centerline.

5. Following figure 2, stitch another polystar pattern, taking the stitches below the pins at the centerline and into the space of the pattern already worked. This pattern will overlap into the bottom half of the ball.

6. Repeat step 5 on the bottom half of the ball. Continue to work this way, alternating rounds from top to bottom and changing colors as desired, until you have the number of bands you need. Note that a diamond shape will form where the threads cross at the centerline.

Figure 1

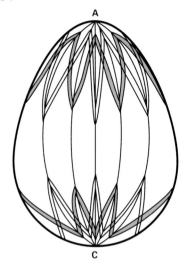

Figure 2

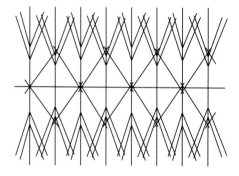

Egg Pattern 2

Similar to the first egg pattern, this design is worked on a smaller shape that is 3 inches (7.5 cm) in length, and uses pearl cotton (coton perlé) #8 (coton á broder) for the pattern thread.

MATERIALS

- 3-inch (7.5 cm) polystyrene egg
- White polyester sewing thread, 325 yards (300 m)
- Silver metallic thread, 6½ yards (6 m)
- Pearl cotton (coton perlé) #8 (coton á broder), 9 yards (8 m) each of red and emerald green

INSTRUCTIONS

1. Wrap the egg and divide it into 12 vertical sections with a line around the center. Using the metallic thread, apply the guidelines.

2. Work the polystar pattern around the shape on the first set of guidelines. Work around the top point first. Stitch the pattern until it is approximately ⅜ inch (1 cm) from the centerline.

3. Work the next round of the polystar pattern on the guidelines in between those already worked, finishing at the same distance from the centerline.

4. Repeat steps 2 and 3 around the bottom point of the ball.

5. Finish off around the center following steps 5 and 6 for Egg Pattern 1 on page 121. You can also finish the ball by following figure 1 to plot points by placing pins approximately 1 inch (2.5 cm) from the top and bottom pins. These will be within the space created between the two bands of the polystar patterns. Stitch the polystar pattern from the pins at the top of the ball to the pins at the bottom of the ball. As shown in the diagram, stitch from D to E to F to G, etc. Then work a few rounds on the lines in between those already worked; as in the diagram, stitch from S to T to U to V, etc.

Figure 1

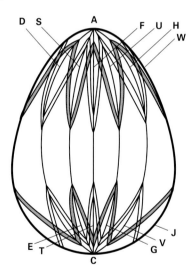

Extended Points

This is a simpler version of the square crossing patterns on pages 36 to 42. While it uses the same stitching pattern, it is not worked around two centers.

MATERIALS

- 3-inch (70-80 mm) ball
- Medium lavender polyester sewing thread, 325 yards (300 m)
- Gold metallic thread, 5½ yards (5 m)
- Fine gold metallic thread, 2¼ yards (2 m)
- Pearl cotton (coton perlé) #5, 1 skein = 27.3 yards (25 m), ¼ skein of black, ½ skein each of green, light purple, and red

INSTRUCTIONS

1. Wrap the ball and divide it into eight vertical sections. Using metallic thread, apply only the vertical guidelines. Do not apply a guideline around the center.

2. Following figure 1, plot points D and E. For D, begin on one of the vertical lines and place a pin on a point that is 1 inch (2.5 cm) from point A. For E, place a pin on a point on the same line as D that is 2½ inches (6.5 cm) from point A.

3. Again following figure 1, begin at point E just below the pin, and take a stitch from right to left. Lay the thread along the guideline as you move the thread up to the pin at point D. Turn the ball so point D faces toward you. Take a stitch from right to left at point D just below the pin. Lay the thread along the guideline as you move the thread up to pin E. Turn the ball so point E faces toward you. Take a stitch from right to left at E below the pin. Repeat step 3 until the stitching above point D reaches point A, changing colors as you wish.

Figure 1

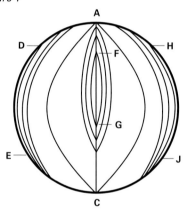

Figure 2

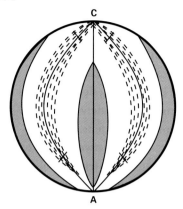

> **TIP:** *Always make sure that the point around which you are stitching faces toward you. As you take each stitch around the pins at the points, do not let them get too close to each other or the thread along the guidelines will not lie smoothly.*

4. Plot points F and G, H and J, and K and L as you did for points D and E in step 2. Work this same pattern between points F and G, and H and J, as shown in figure 1, and on points K and L on the other side of the ball. Note that, though not shown, points K and L correspond to points F and G on the other side of the ball.

5. Once you've completed steps 2 to 4, turn the ball so that C is at the top. Repeat steps 2 to 4 on the guidelines that do not have stitching as shown in figure 2.

6. Using the fine metallic thread, decorate the area around points A and C with the star motif.

Wrapped Layer Highlights

This design creates open spaces between pattern threads that allow you to experiment with multi-color effects on the wrapping layer. Working on a smaller 2-inch (50 mm) ball, and using the #5 pearl cotton (coton perlé) as shown here, also provides a different outcome than you would get using thinner pearl cotton (coton perlé) #8 (coton á broder) for your pattern thread.

MATERIALS

2- or 2½-inch (50-65 mm) ball

Dark turquoise, 217 yards (200 m)

Gold metallic thread, 2¼ yards (2 m)

Fine gold metallic thread, 21½ yards (20 m)

Pearl cotton (coton perlé) #5, 1 skein = 27.3 yards
(25 m), ¼ skein each of light blue and light pink

INSTRUCTIONS

1. Wrap the ball. Note how the wrapping layer uses two different colors of thread. The darker color was applied first to make a nice thick base, then the fine gold thread was used to add sparkle. Divide the ball into 12 vertical sections with a line around the center. Using metallic thread, apply the guidelines.

2. Following figure 1, plot points D, E, F, G, H, and J, placing the pins on the center guideline.

3. Again following figure 1, plot points K, L, M, N, O, and P, placing the pins in between guidelines AD, AE, AF, AG, AH and AJ, two-thirds of the distance from point A to the center guideline.

4. Following figure 2, which shows a top view of the ball, enter the wrapped layer with the needle and thread so the needle exits close to point D, just below the pin at the center guideline and to the left of guideline AD. Take the thread up to point K and lay it alongside and to the right of guideline KAN. Take the thread around the pin at point N to point H. Take a stitch at H, right to left, just below the pin. Take the thread around the pin at point O, and lay it alongside and to the right of guideline OAL. Take the thread around the pin at point L. Take a stitch at F, right to left, just below the pin. Take the thread around the pin at point M, and lay it alongside and to the right of guideline MAP. Take the thread around the pin at point P and take a stitch at D.

Figure 1

5. Following the same stitching and wrapping pattern as in step 4, work rounds from point E to guideline LAO, to point J to guideline PAM, to point G to guideline NAK, to point E.

6. Turn the ball around so that point C is at the top, and repeat steps 4 and 5. Then repeat steps 4, 5, and 6 once or twice more.

7. Following figure 3, work a herringbone stitch around the center to secure the threads. To do this, begin stitching at point D, then take a stitch at K, this time above the pin, and beneath all the threads. Next take a stitch at these points in this order: E, L, F, M, G, N, H, O, J, P, and D. Figure 3-a shows a detail of the stitching around the centerline.

8. Turn the ball around and repeat step 7 on the other side of the ball. As you can see in figure 3, the stitches at D, E, F, G, H, and J will overlap.

Figure 2

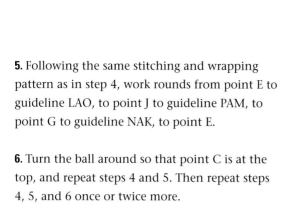

Figure 3

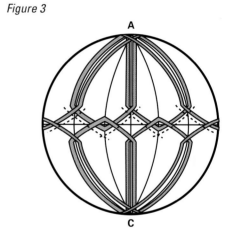

Figure 3-a

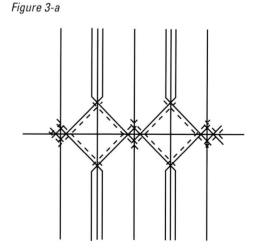

Acknowledgements

To my son Andrew who painstakingly typed all the text for me—a labor of love!!! I would also like to thank Michael Lackie, who devoted much time and thought to the original photographs of my patterns.

Anna Diamond

Having trained as an architect, Anna Diamond spent many years living in the Far East where her work was influenced by the scenery, colors, traditions, and crafts. She enjoys all aspects and techniques of stitching, especially experimenting with colors and textures. She currently teaches and exhibits her work throughout England.